Dear little artists,
This coloring book is dedicated to you, who make the world more colorful with your strokes of joy. May each page be an invitation to unleash your imagination and fill the paper with the happiest colors. Have fun painting and creating!

Digital X
2024

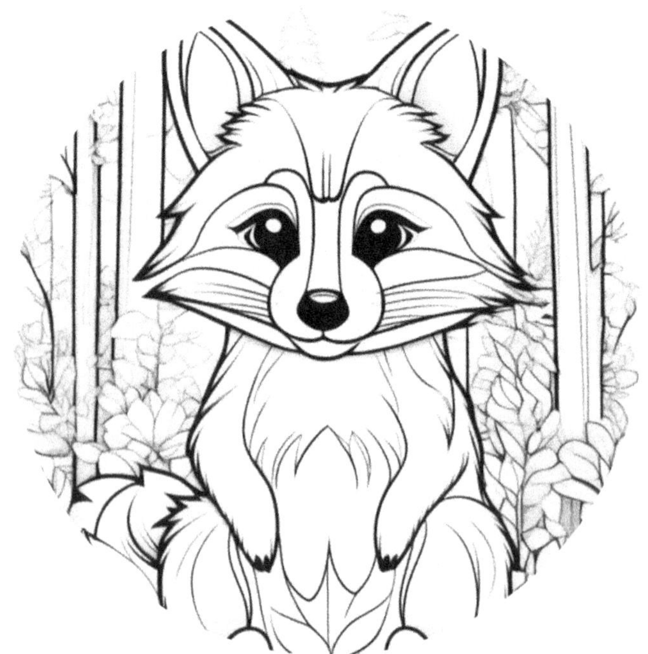

THIS BOOK BELONGS TO:

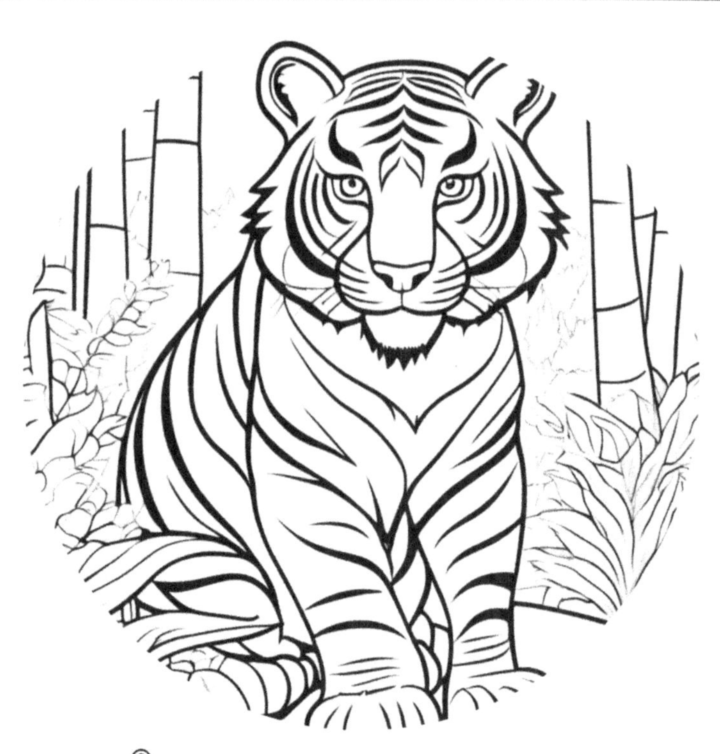

Test Color Page

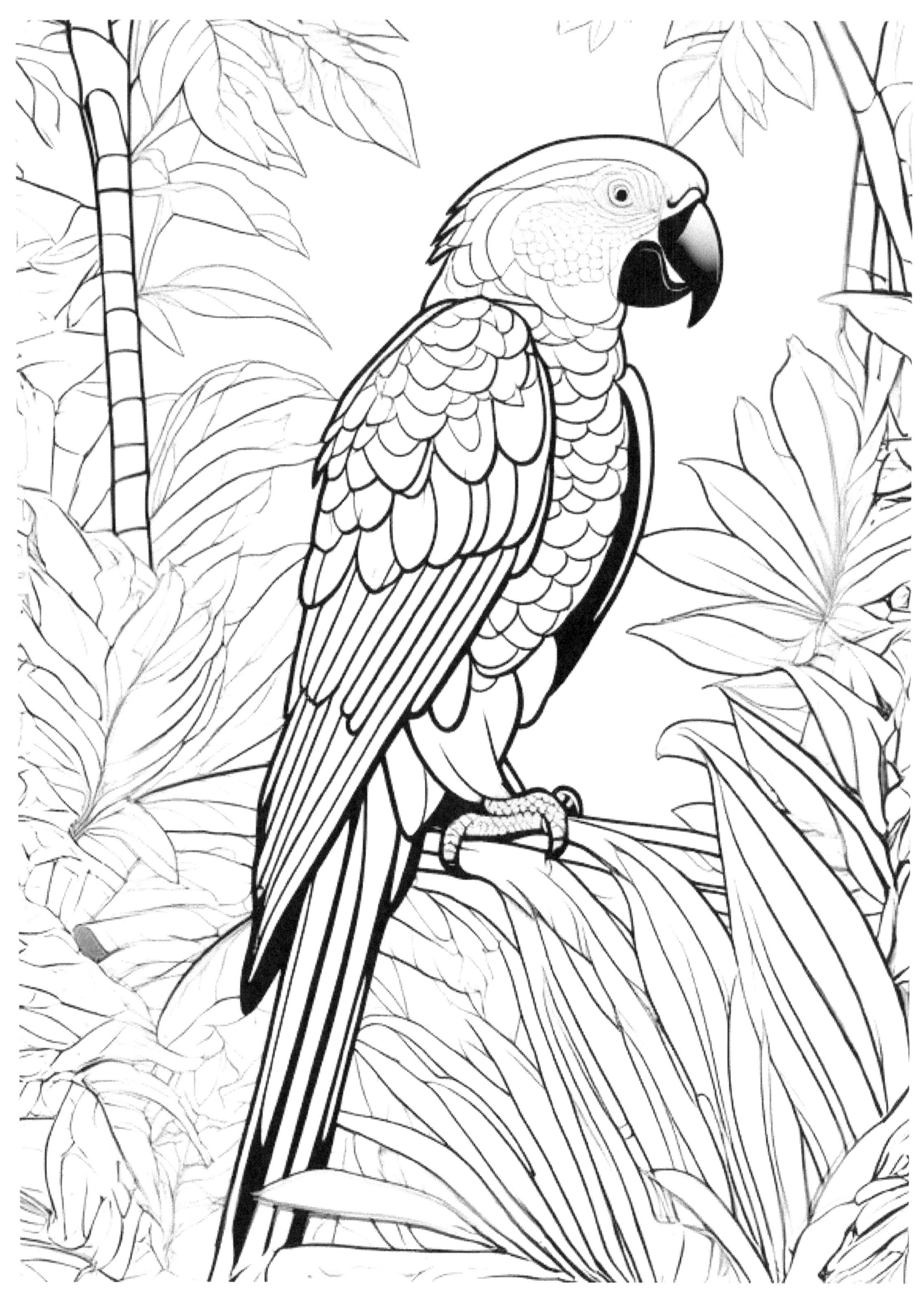

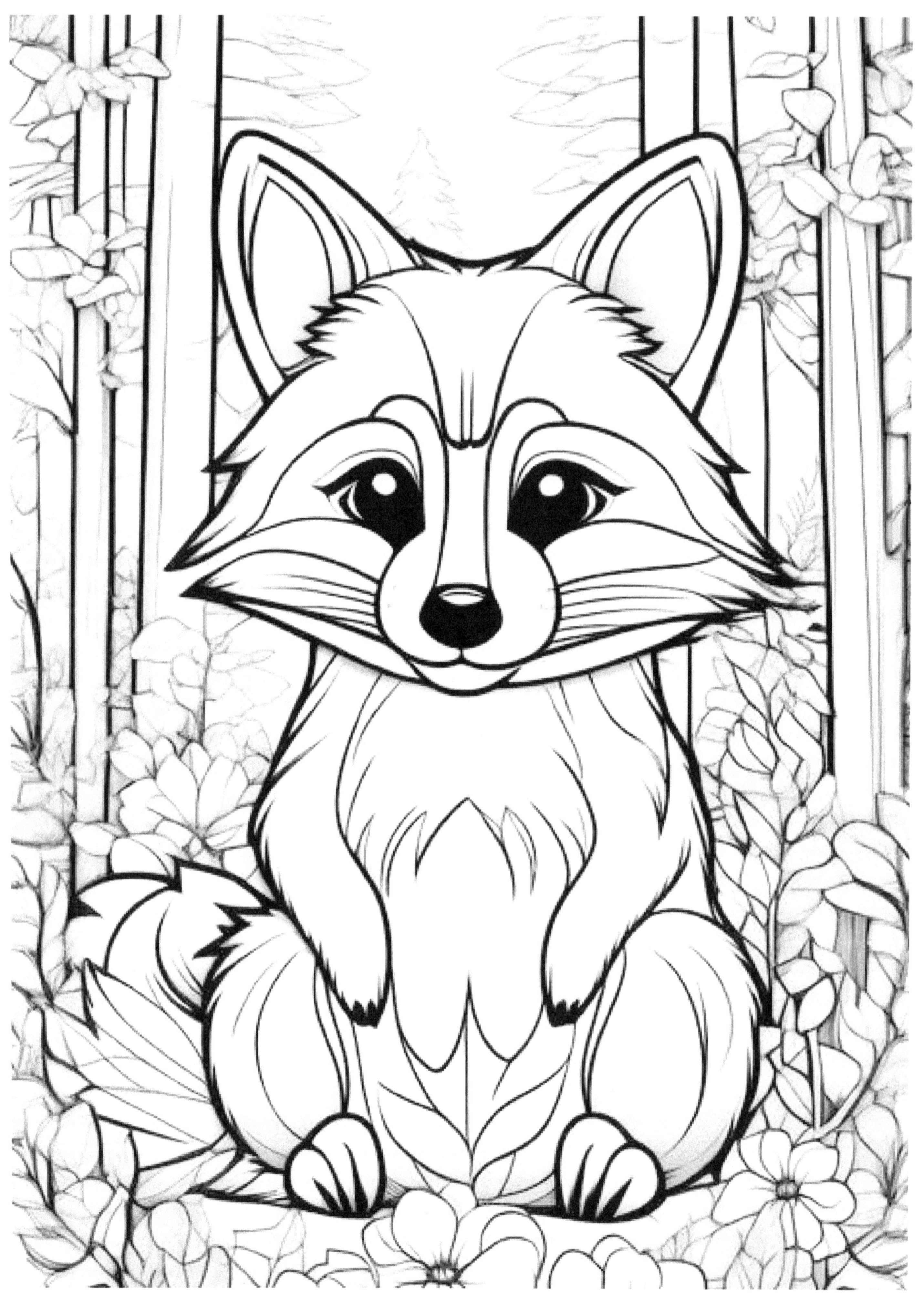

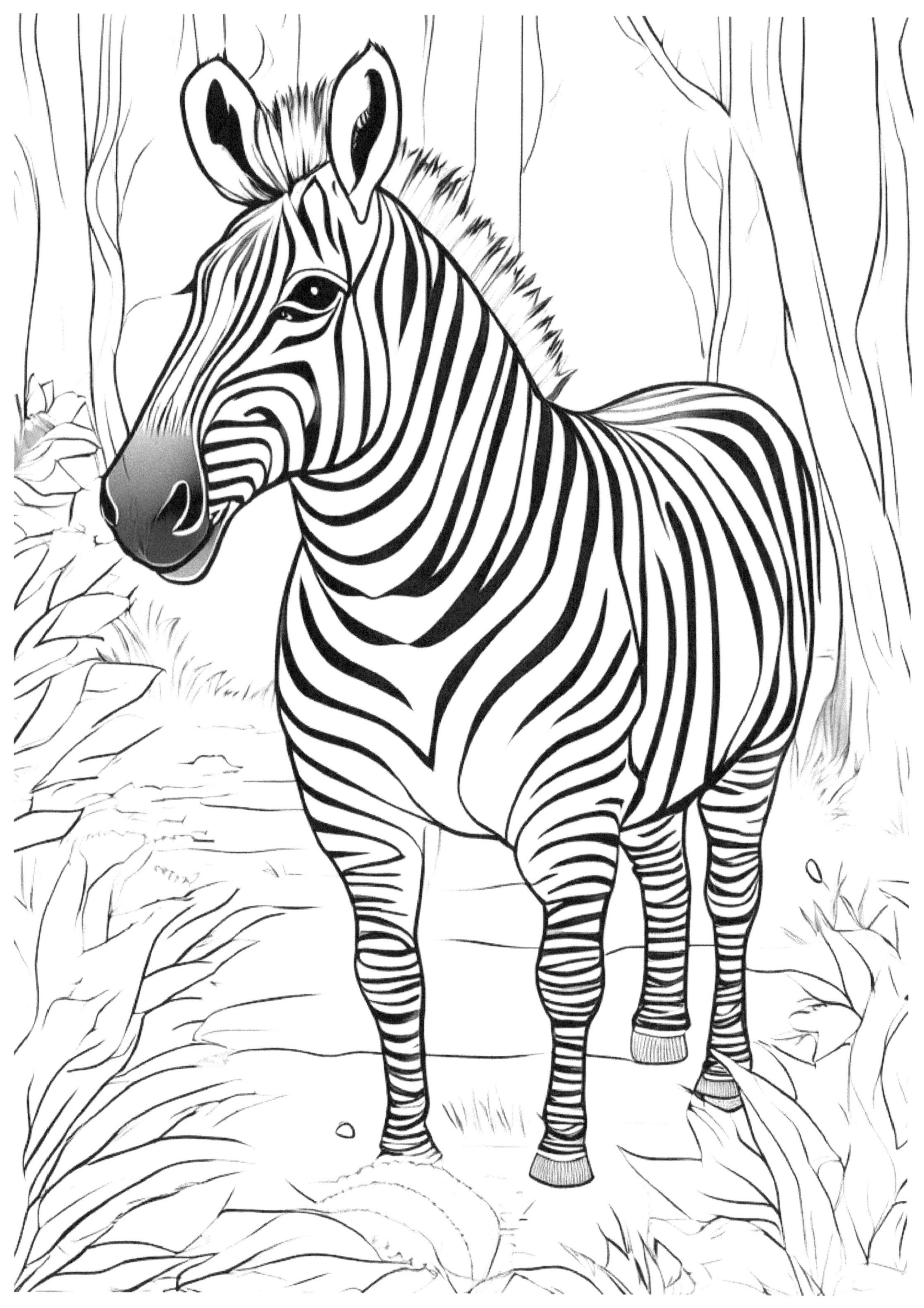

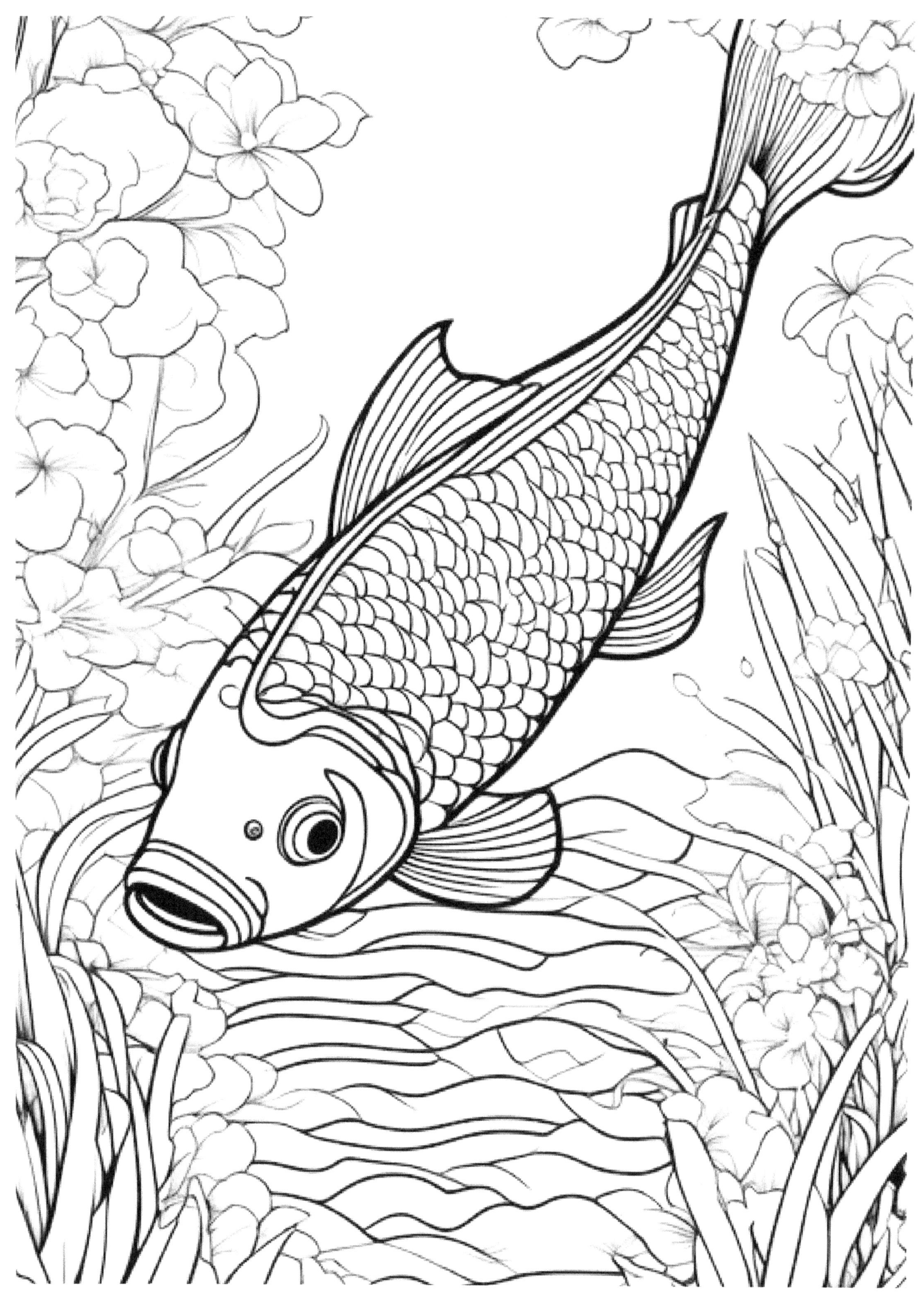

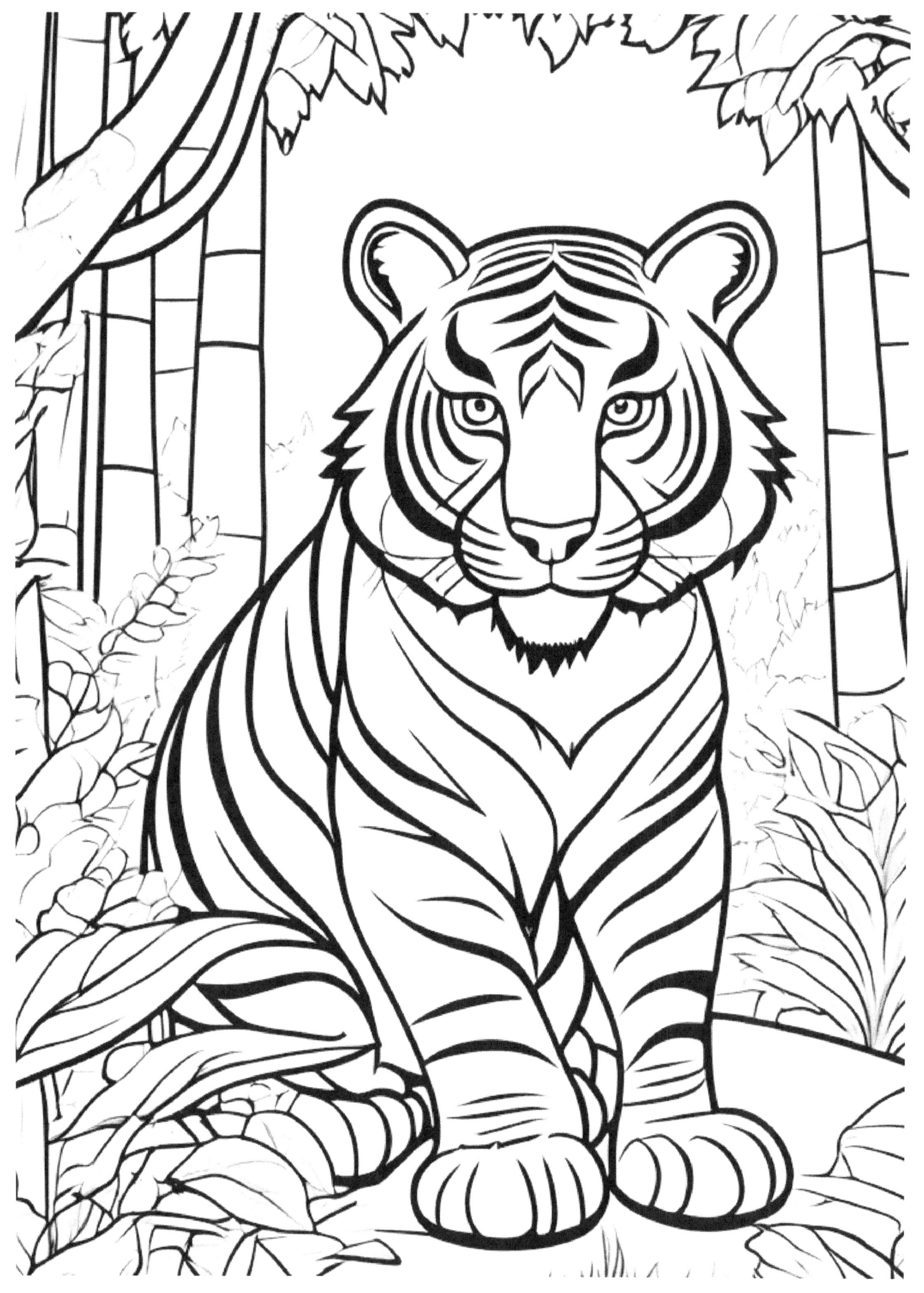

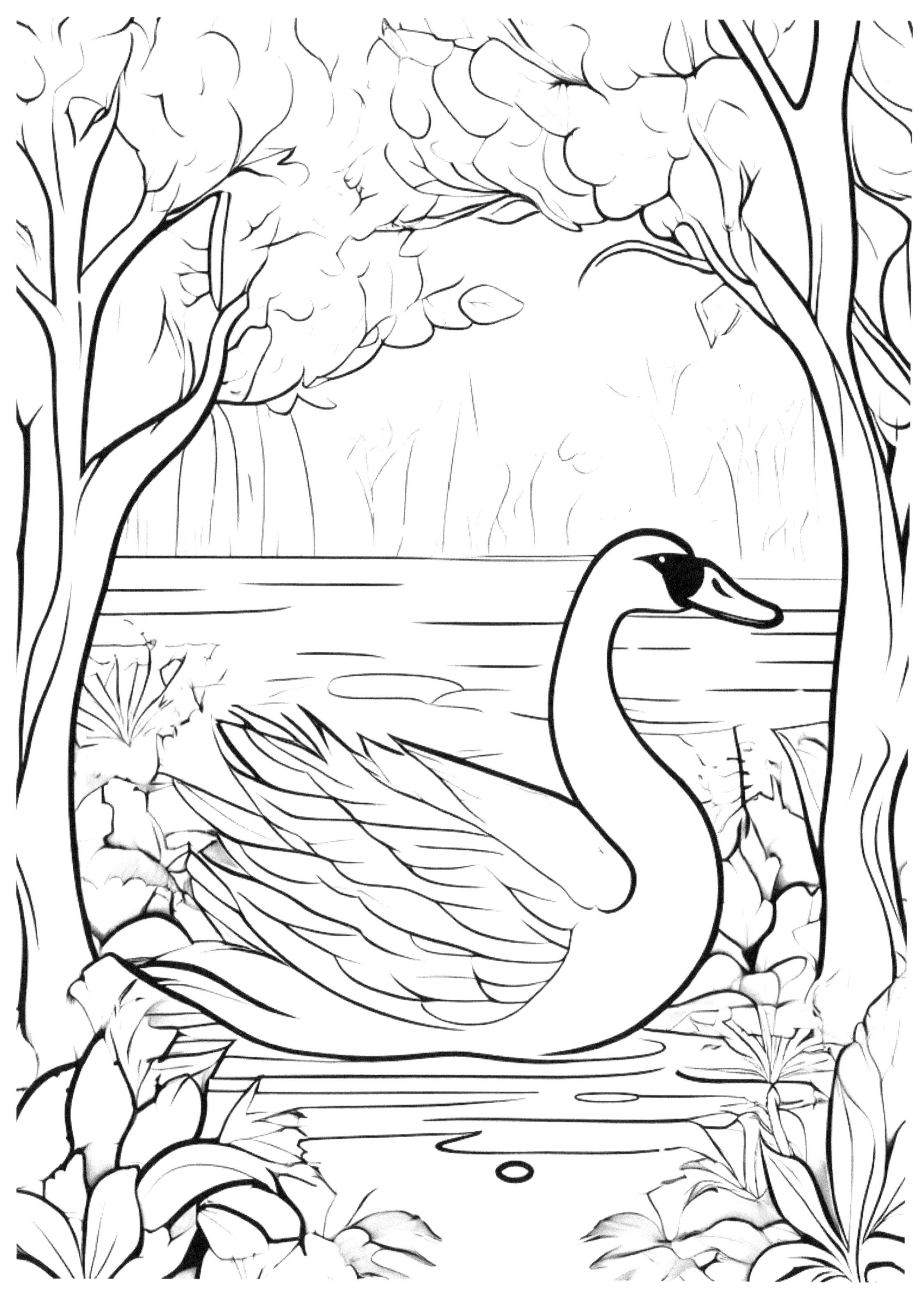

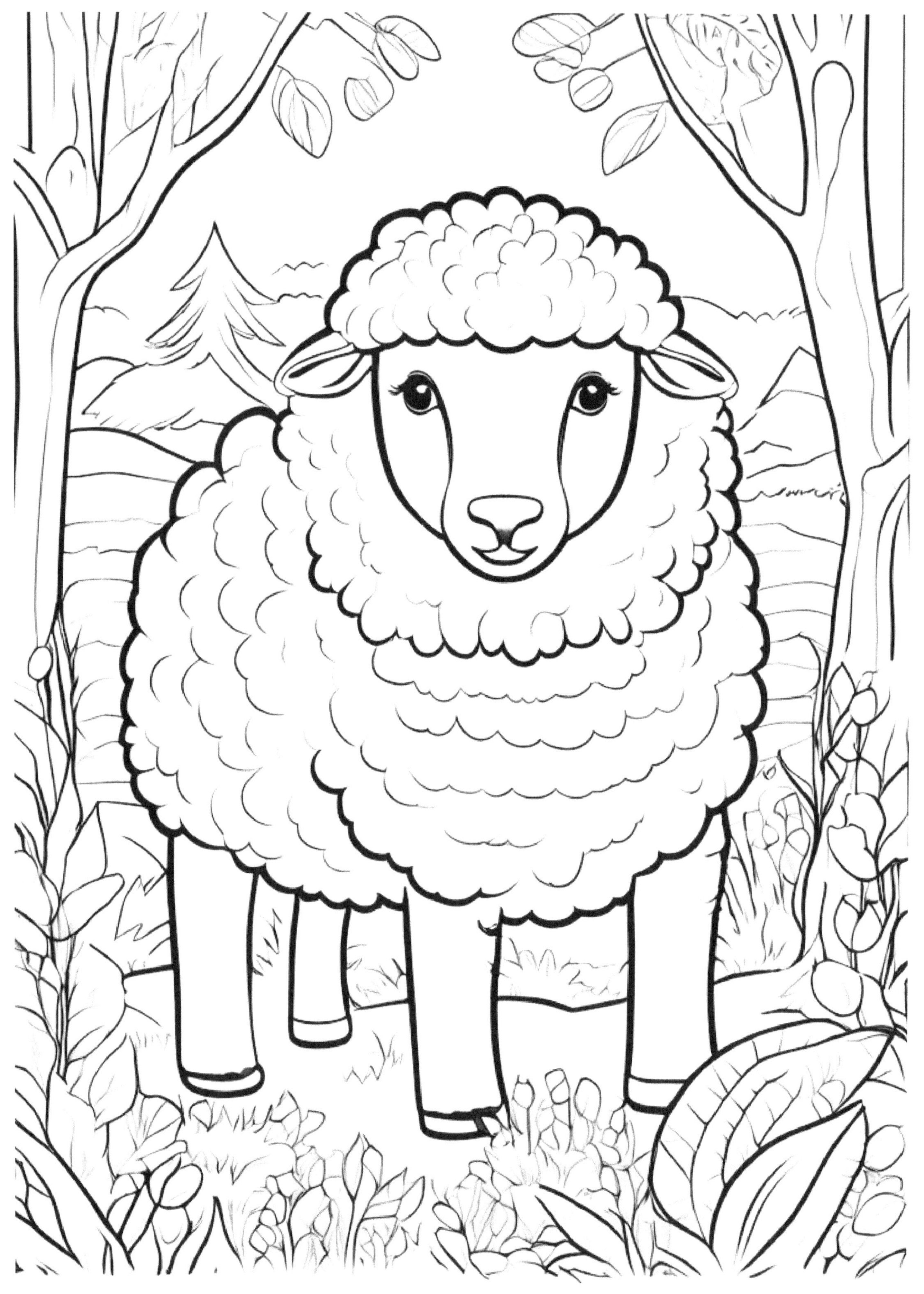

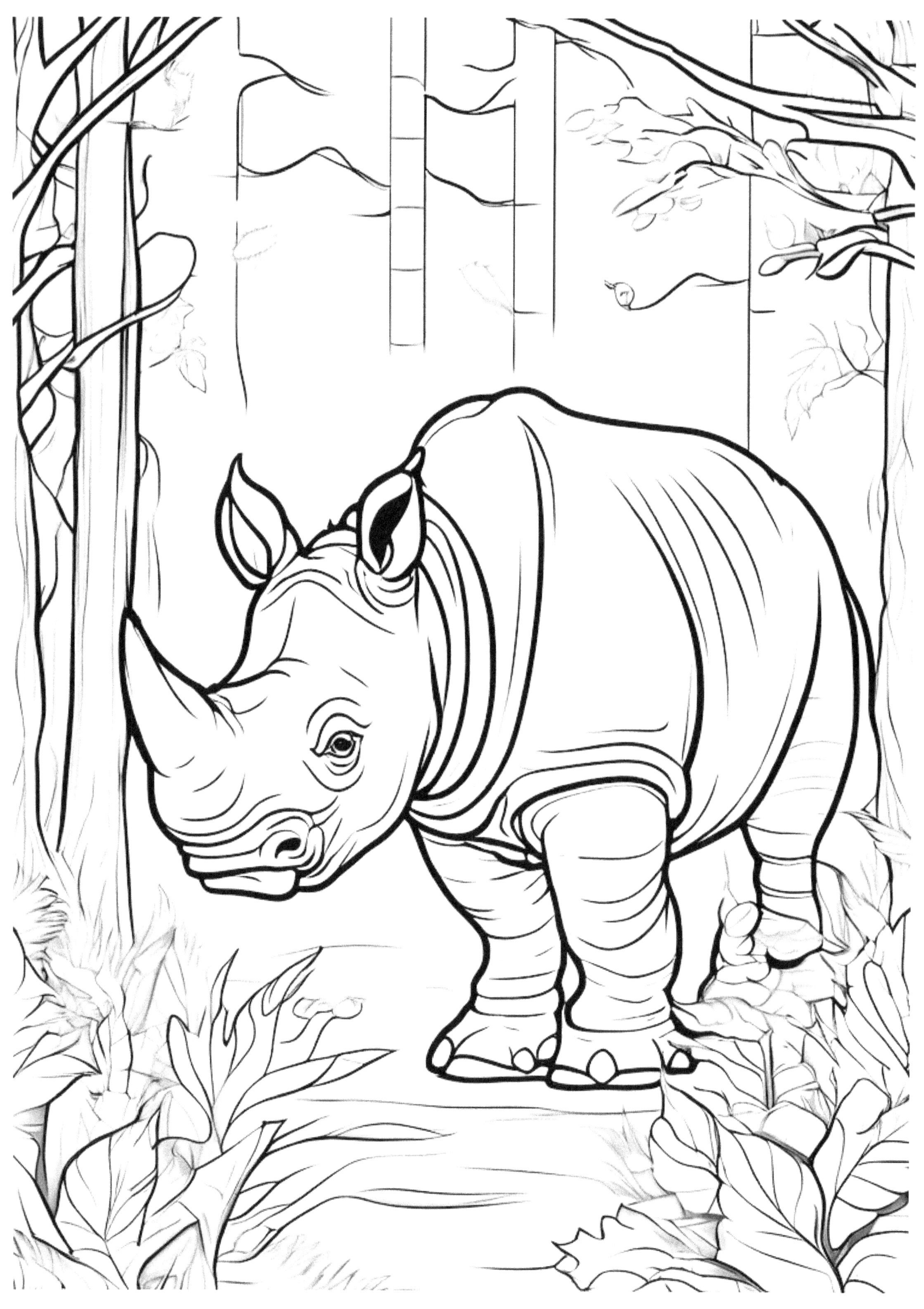

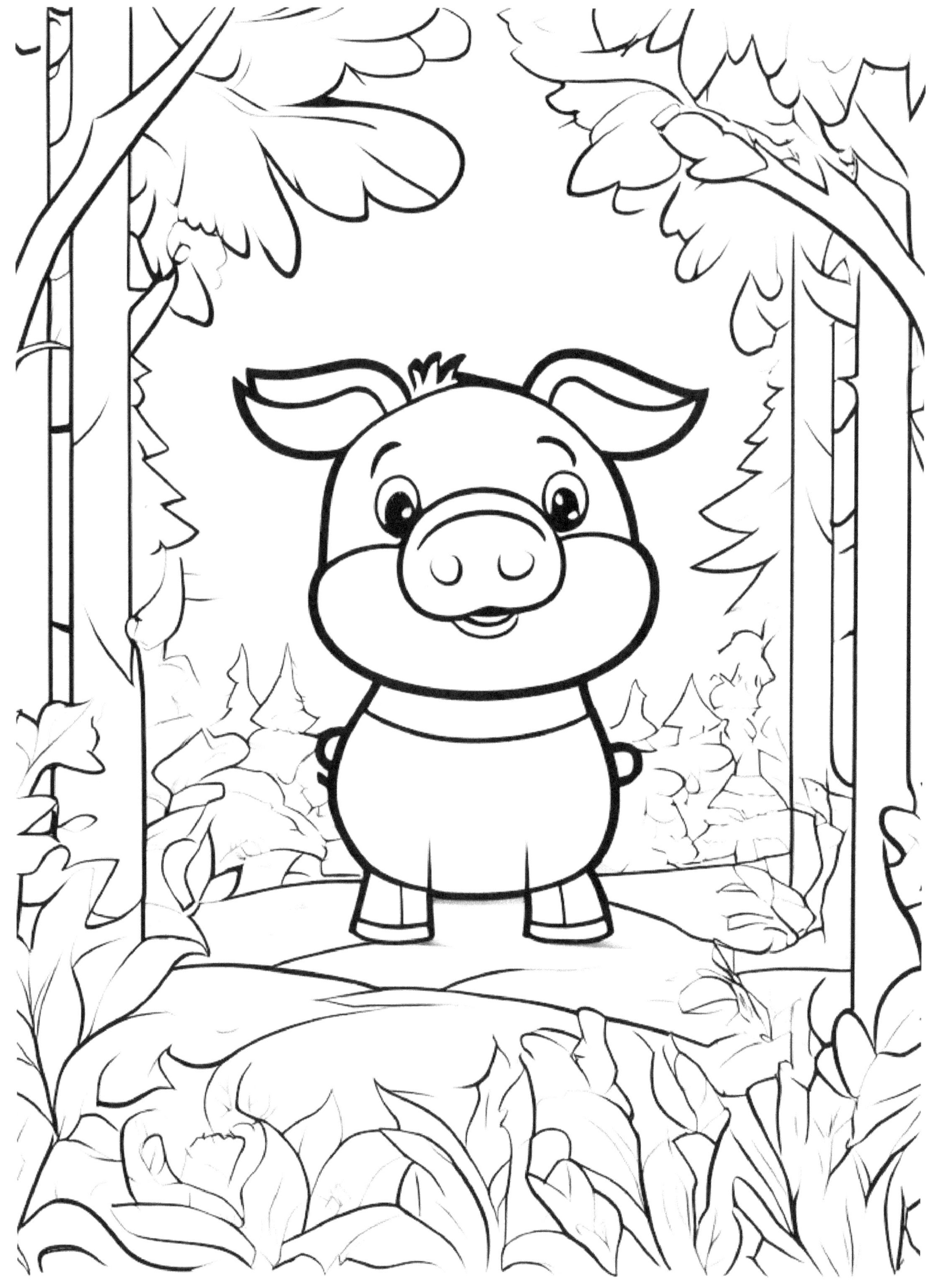

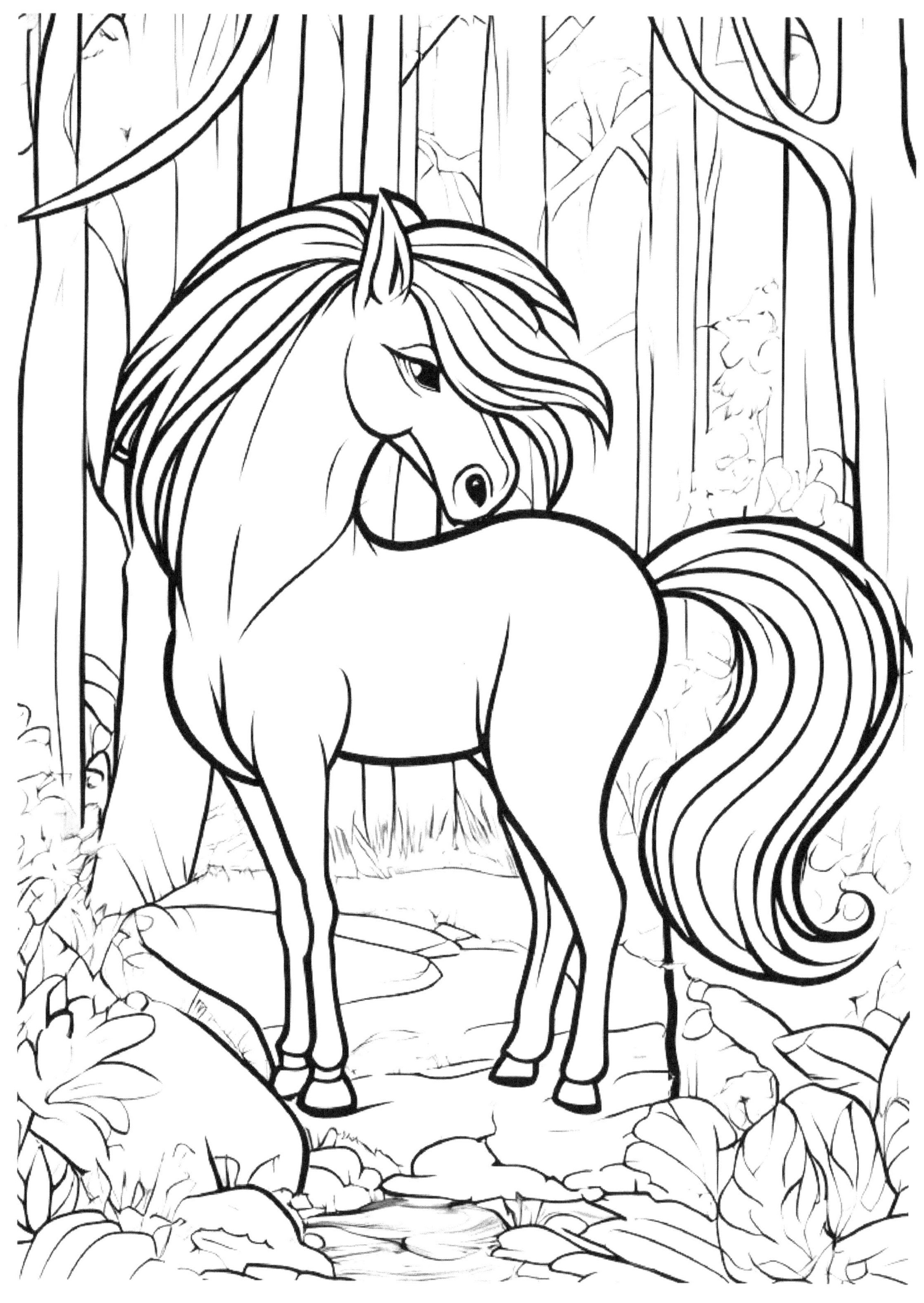

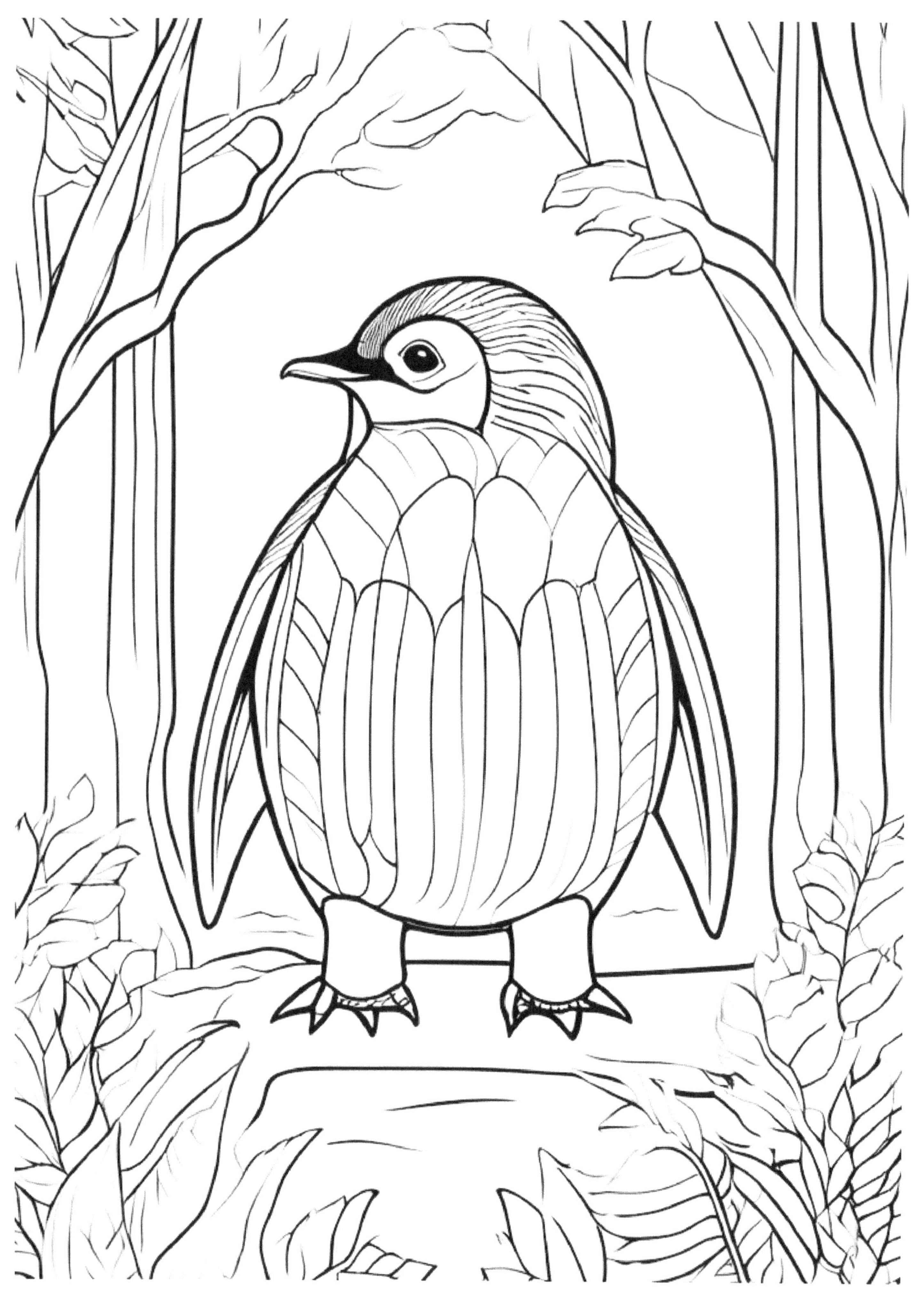

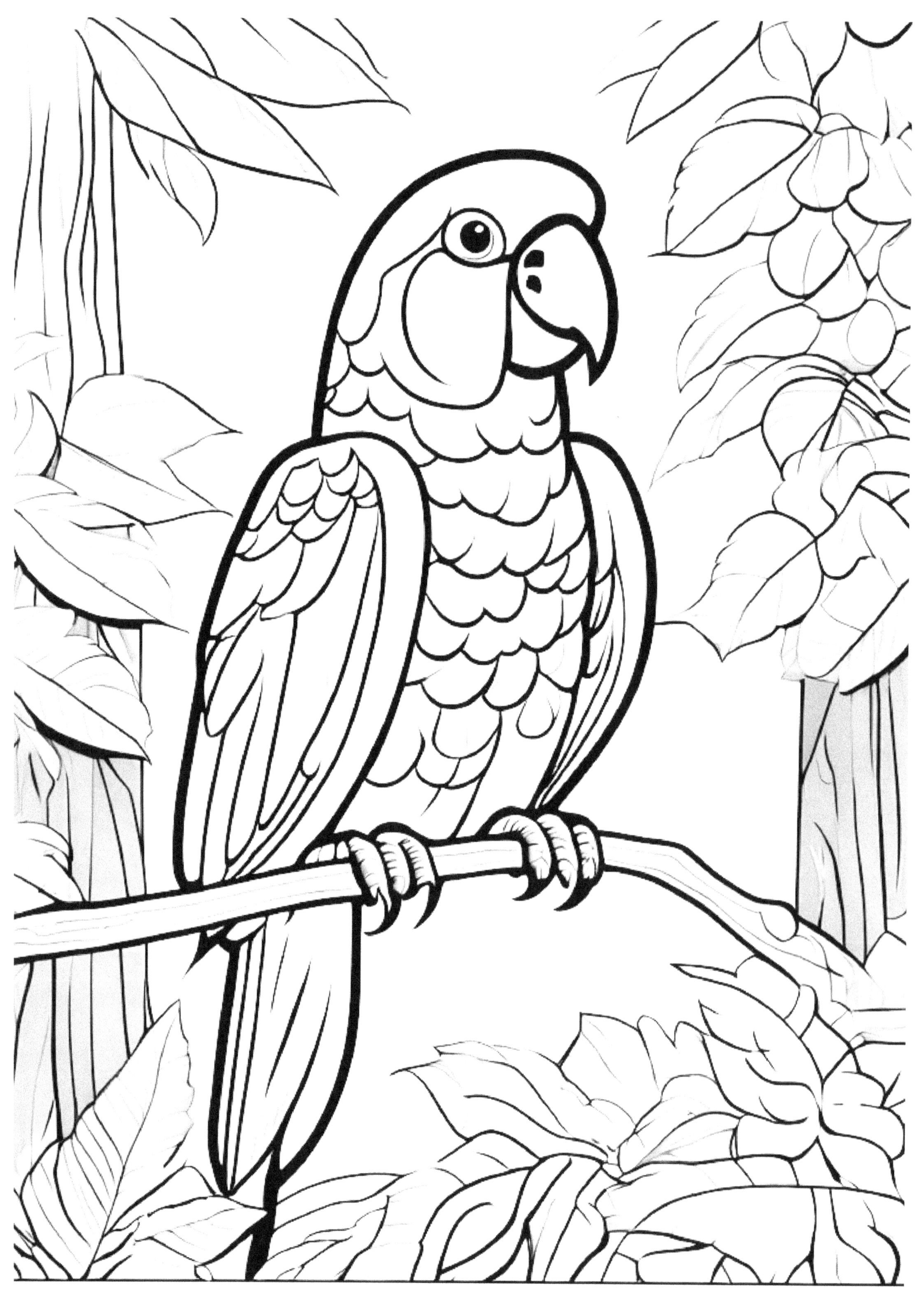

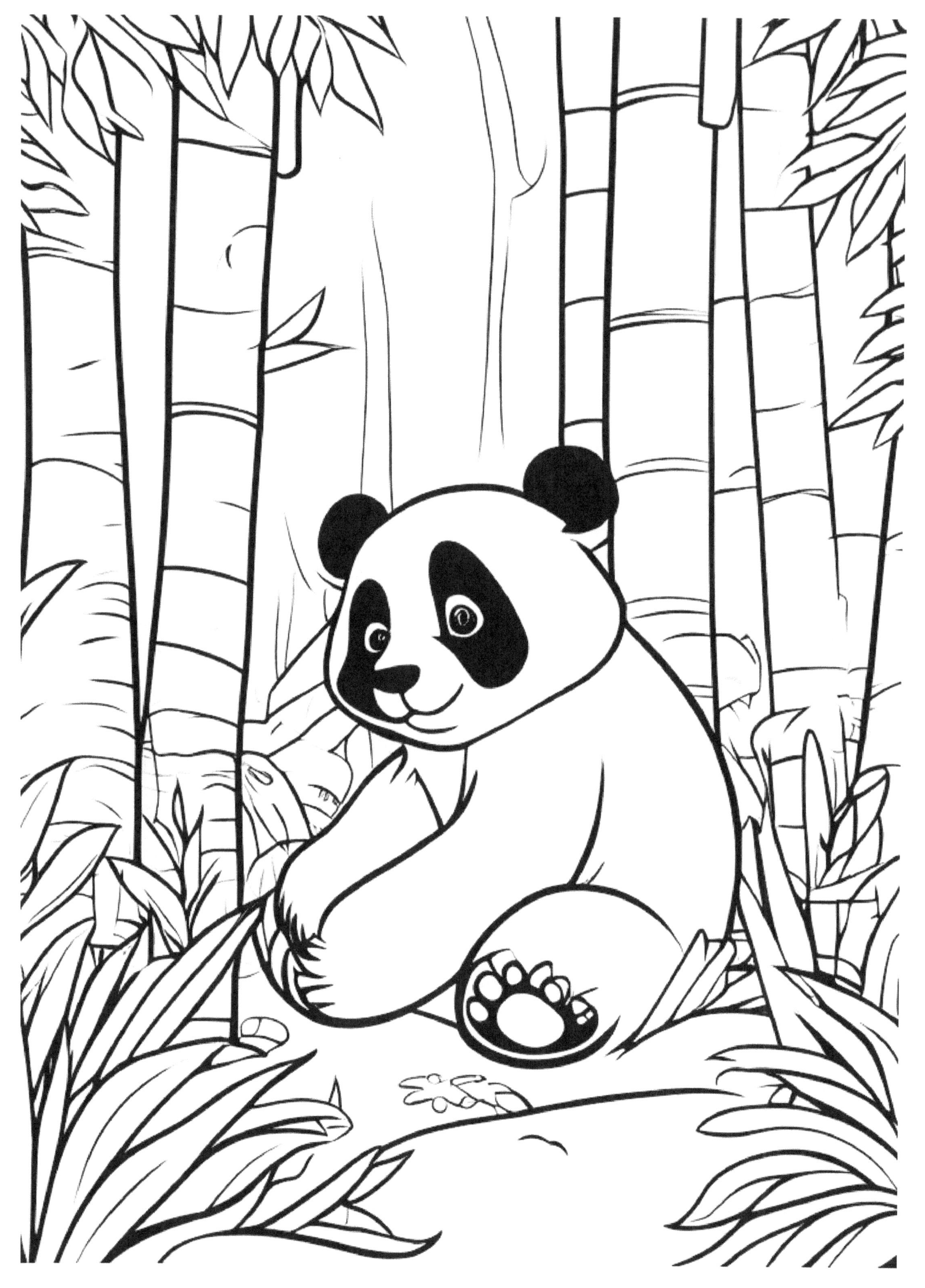

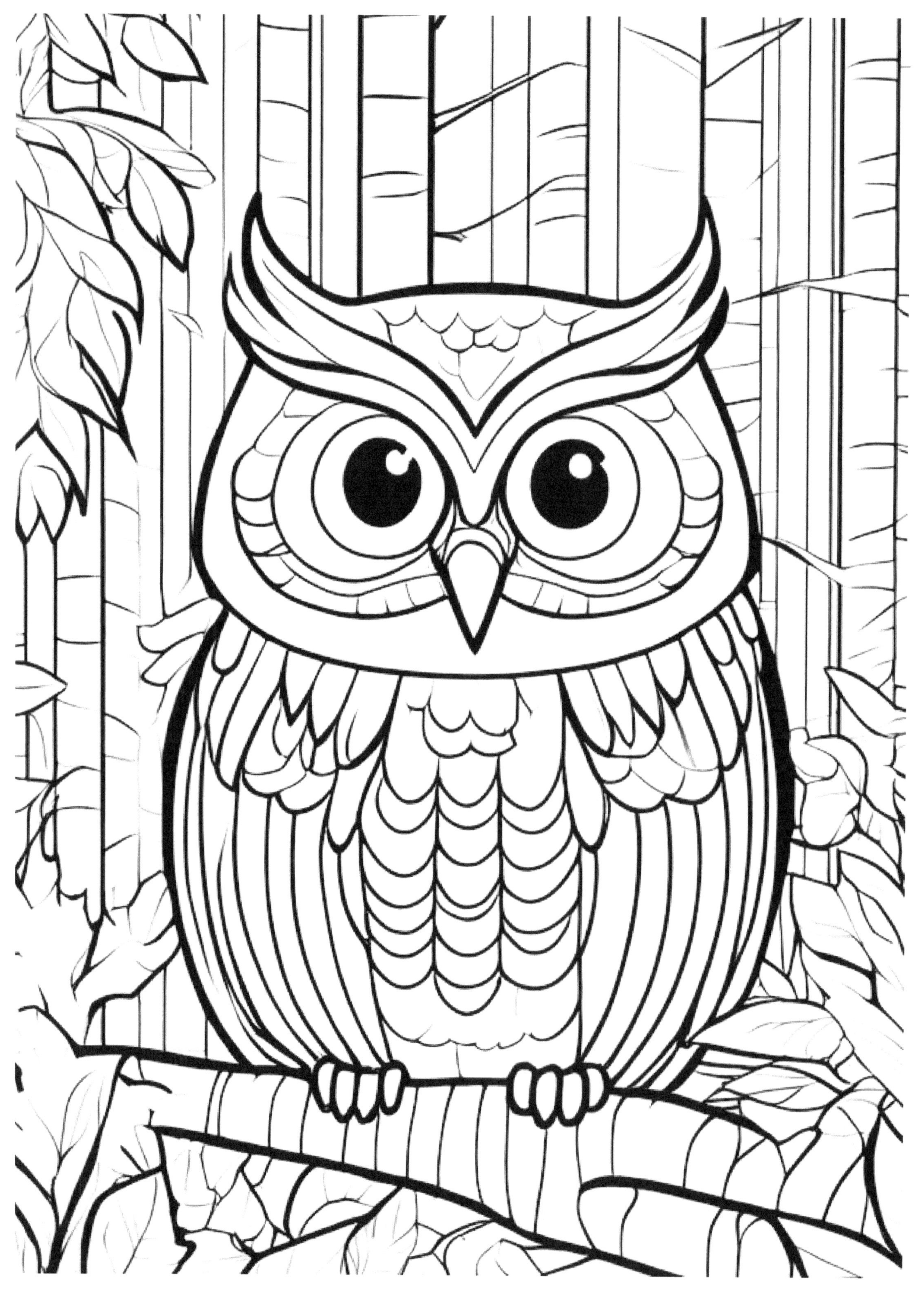

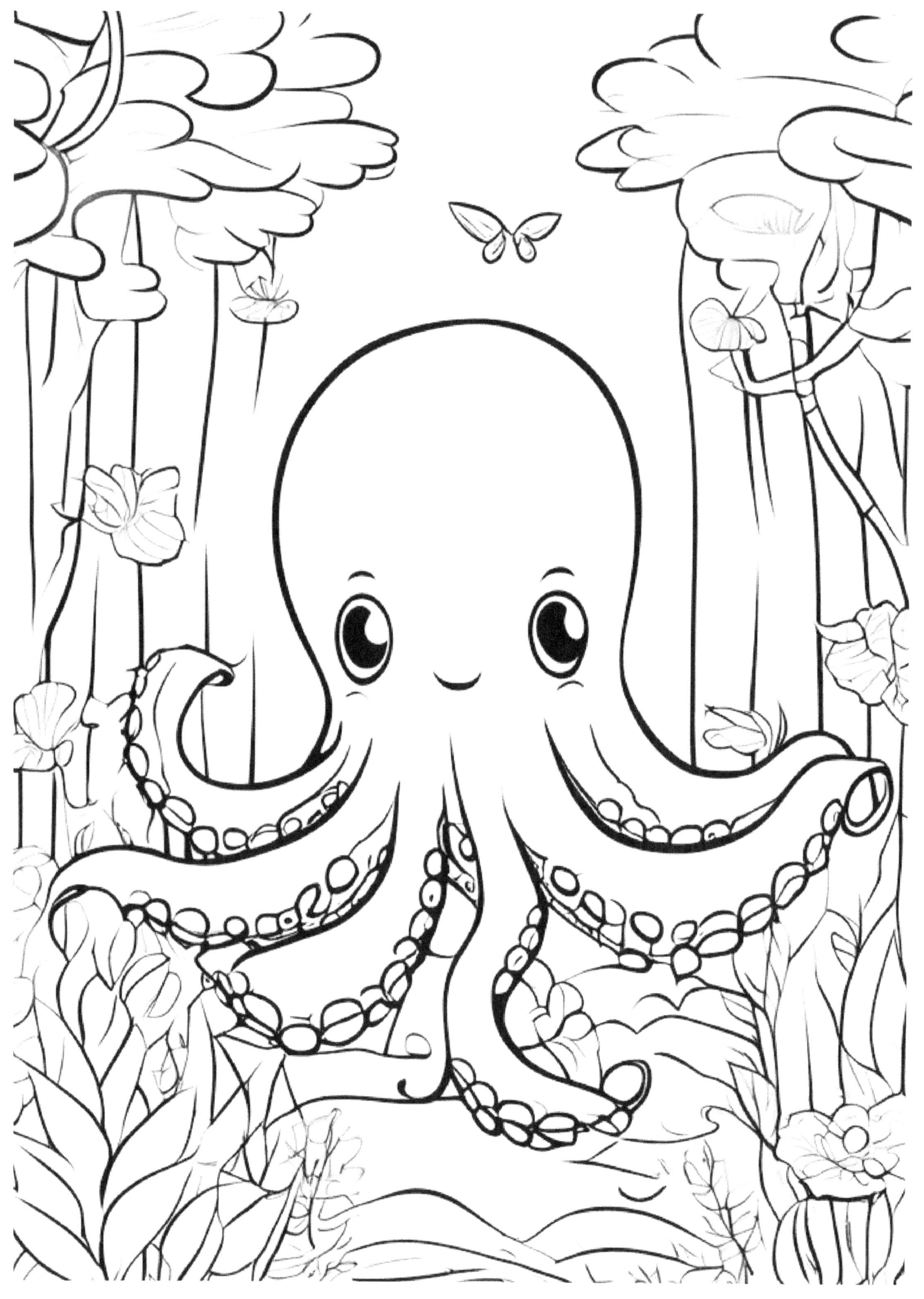

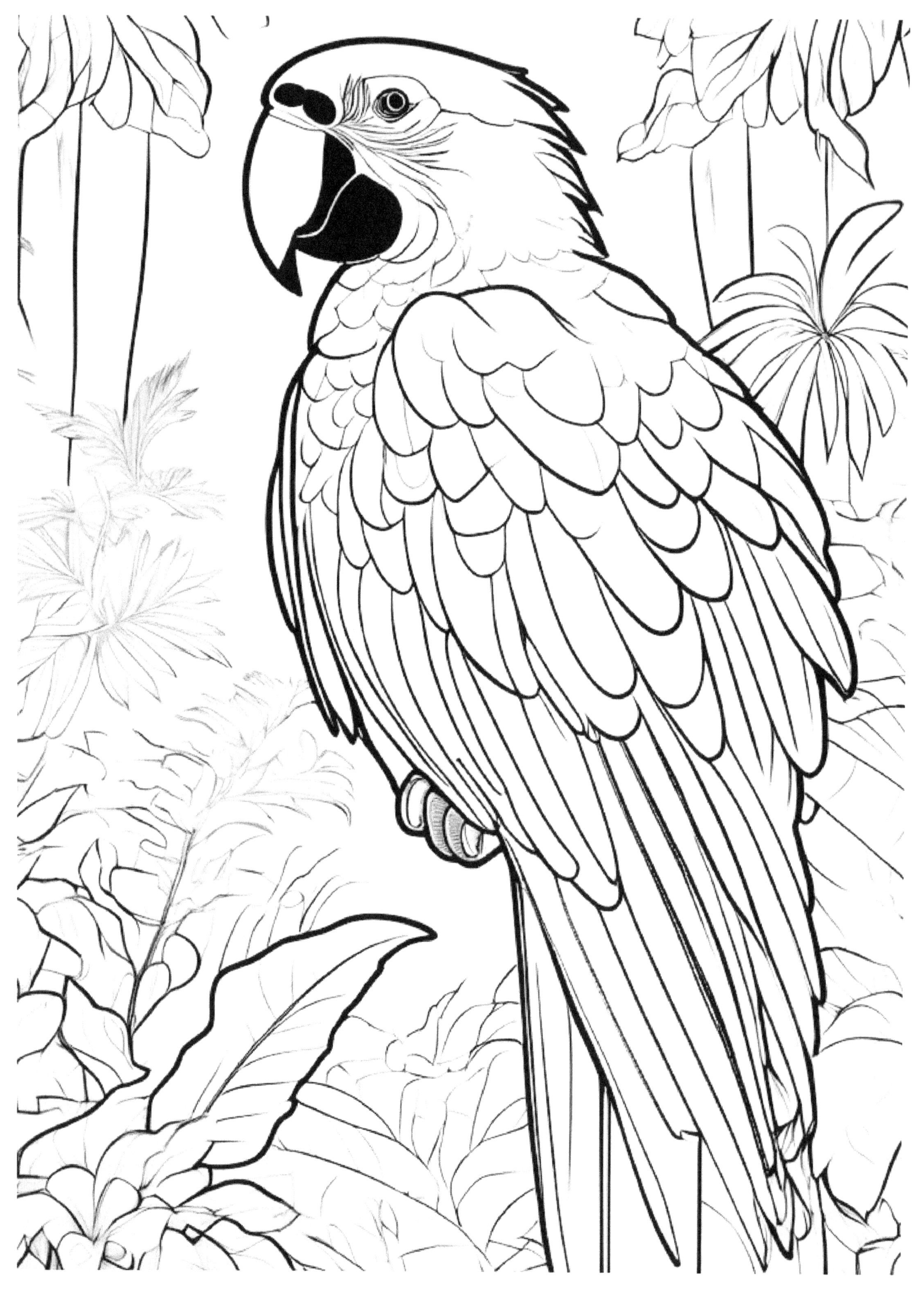

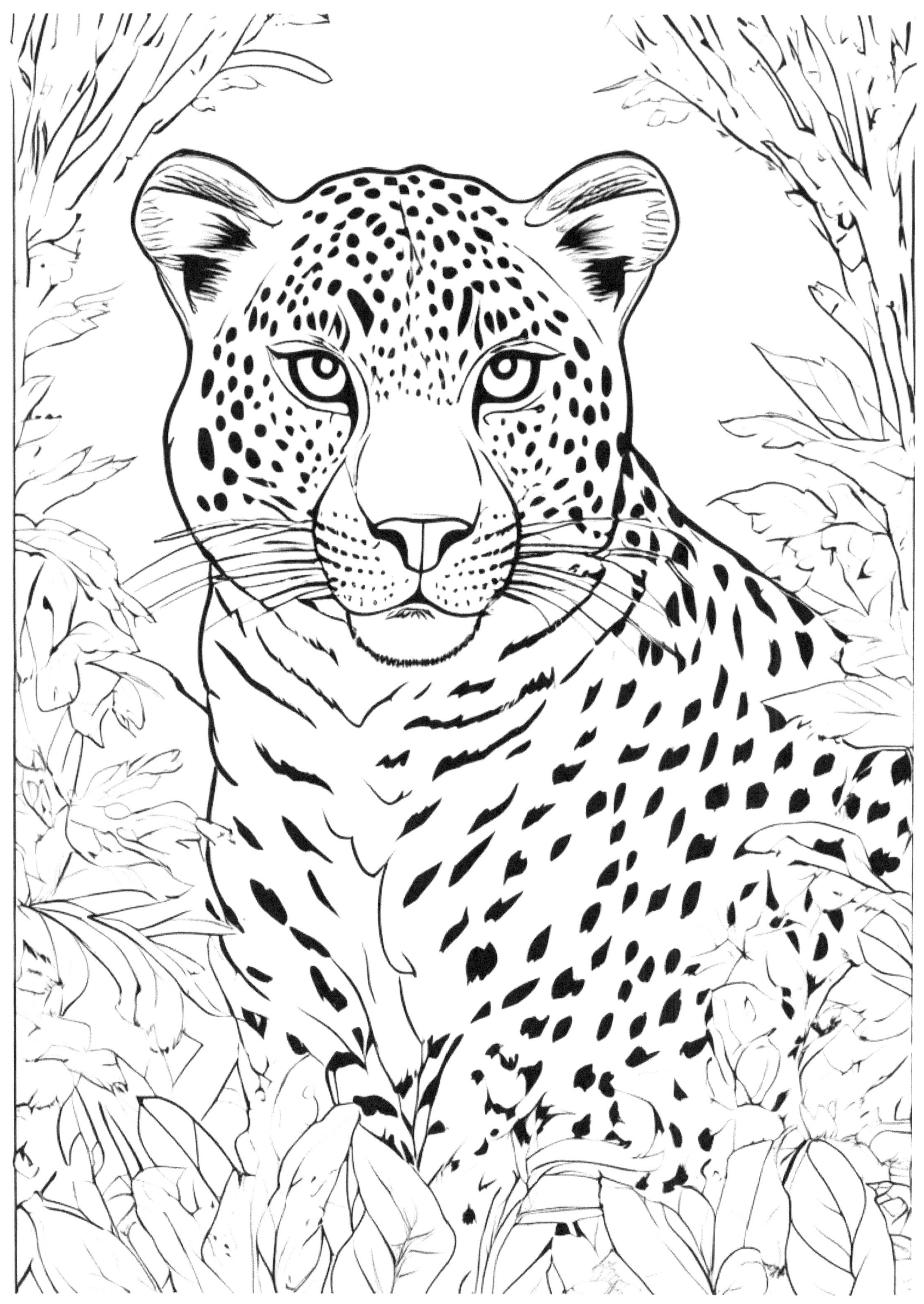

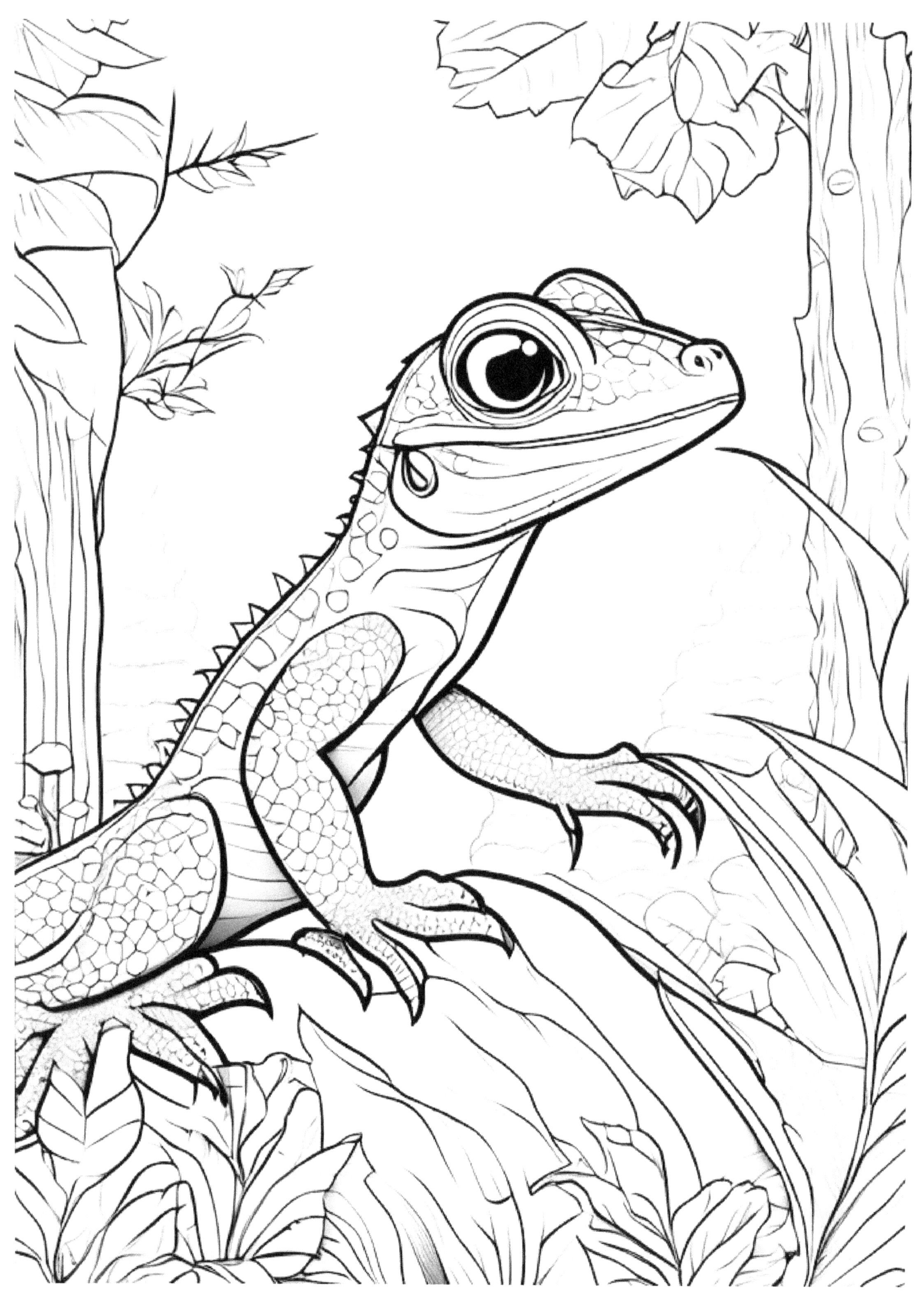

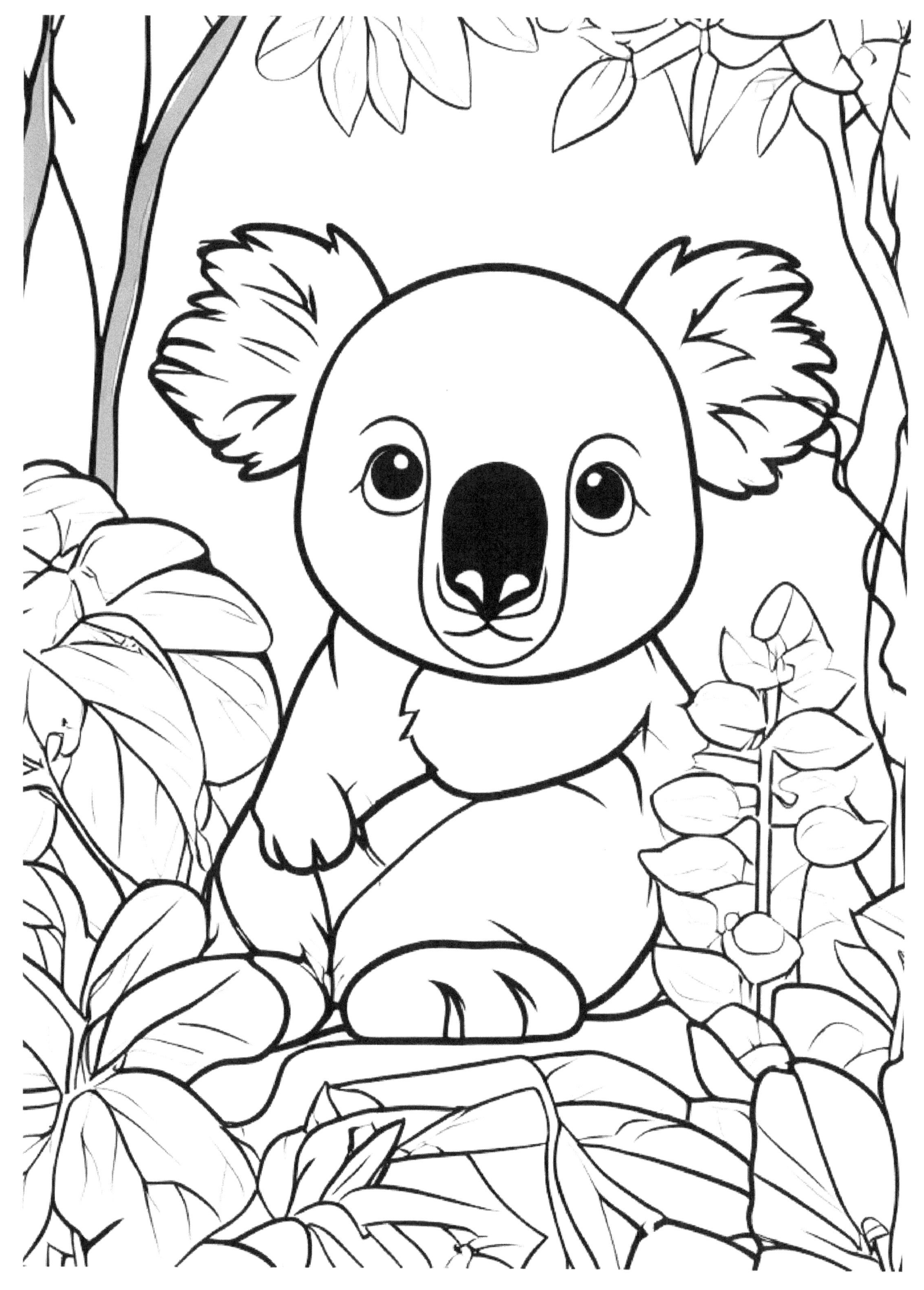

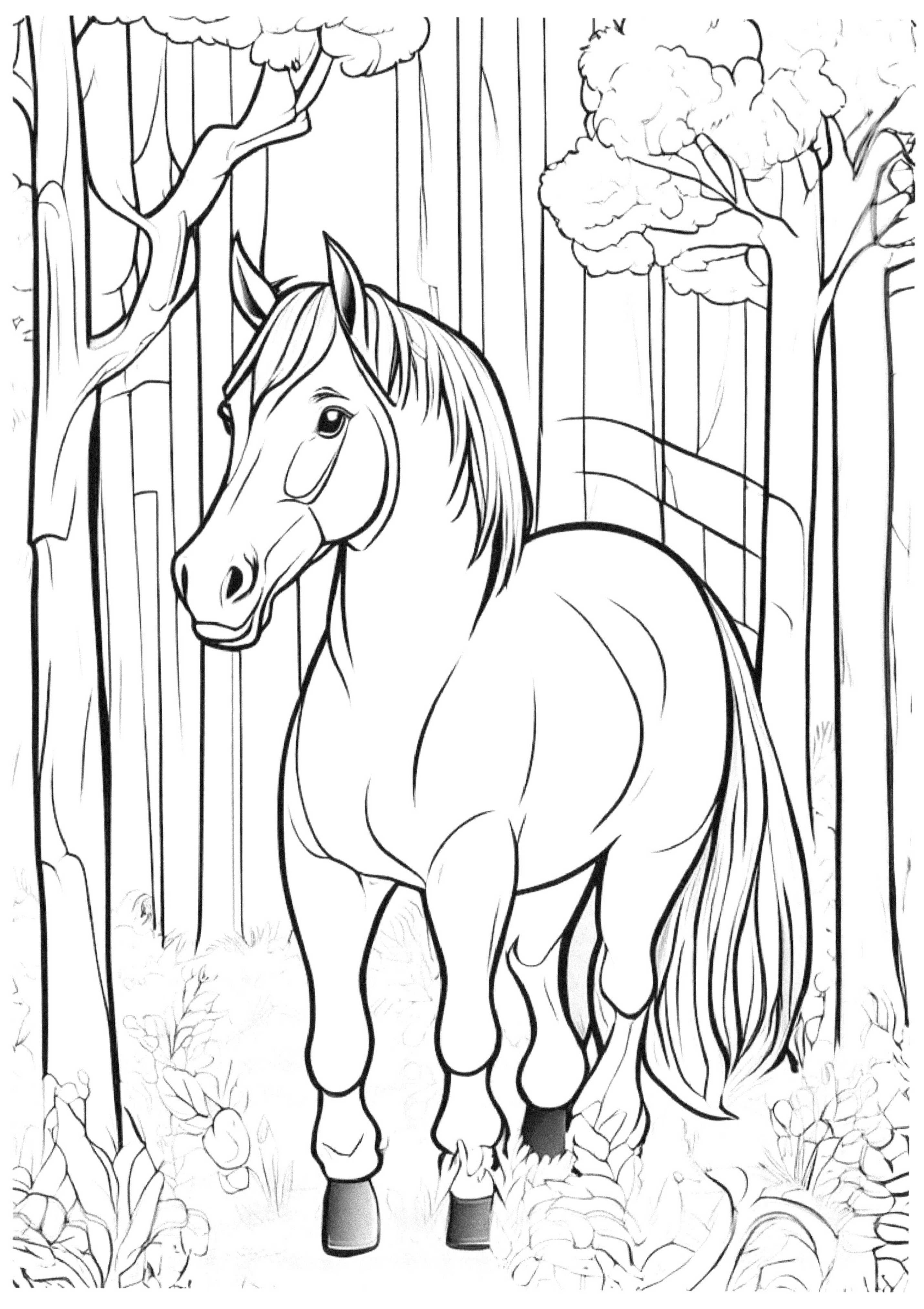

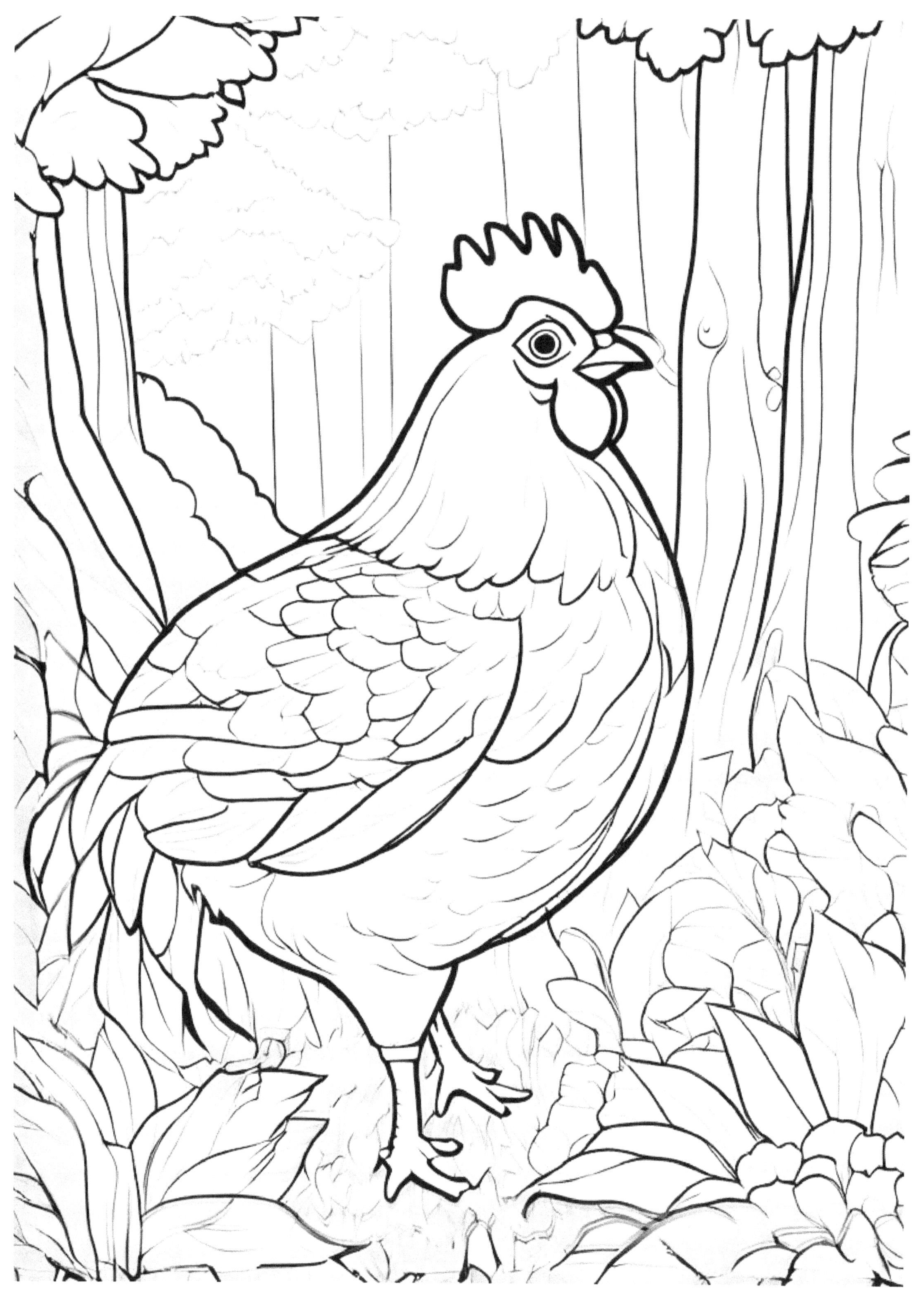

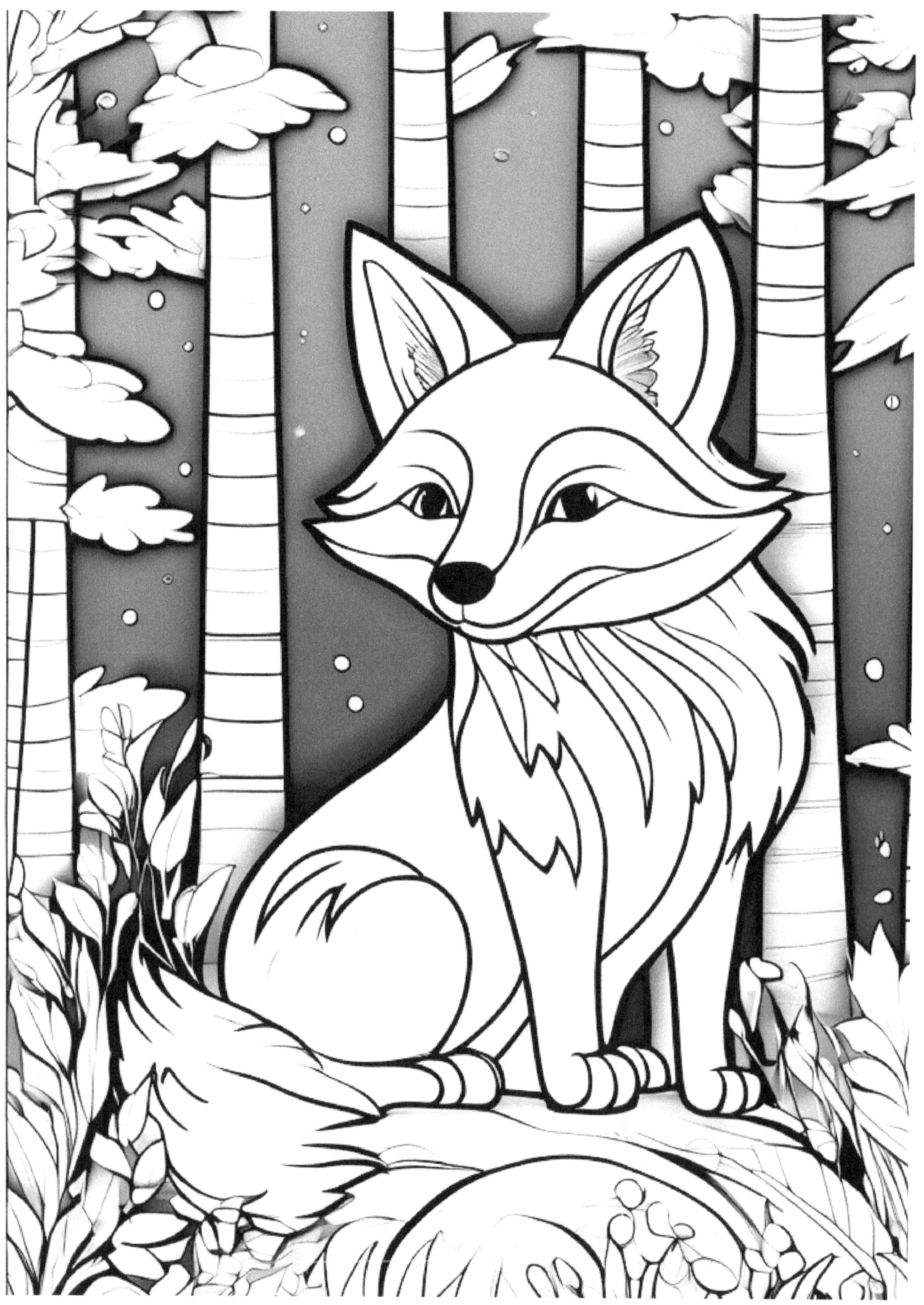

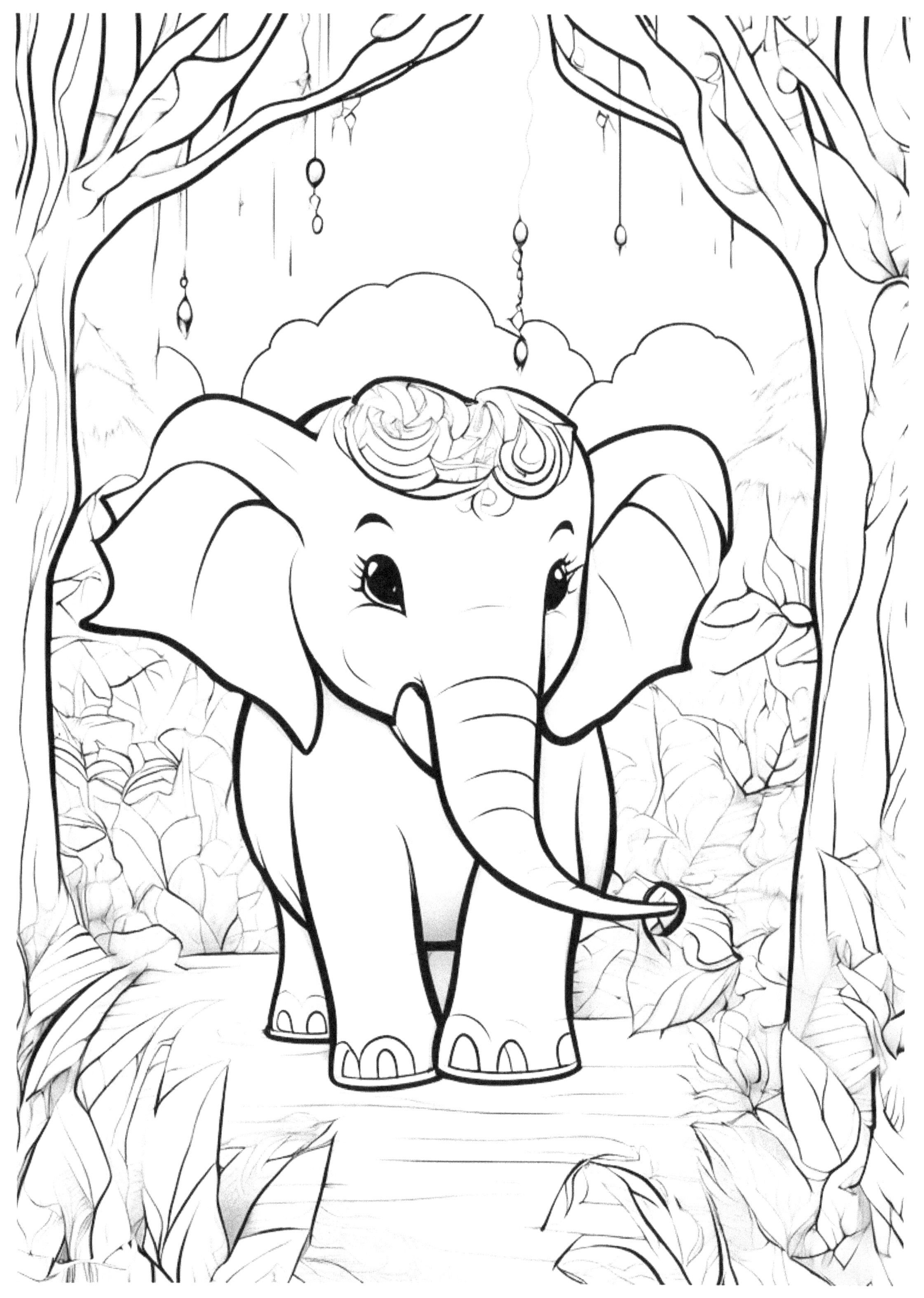

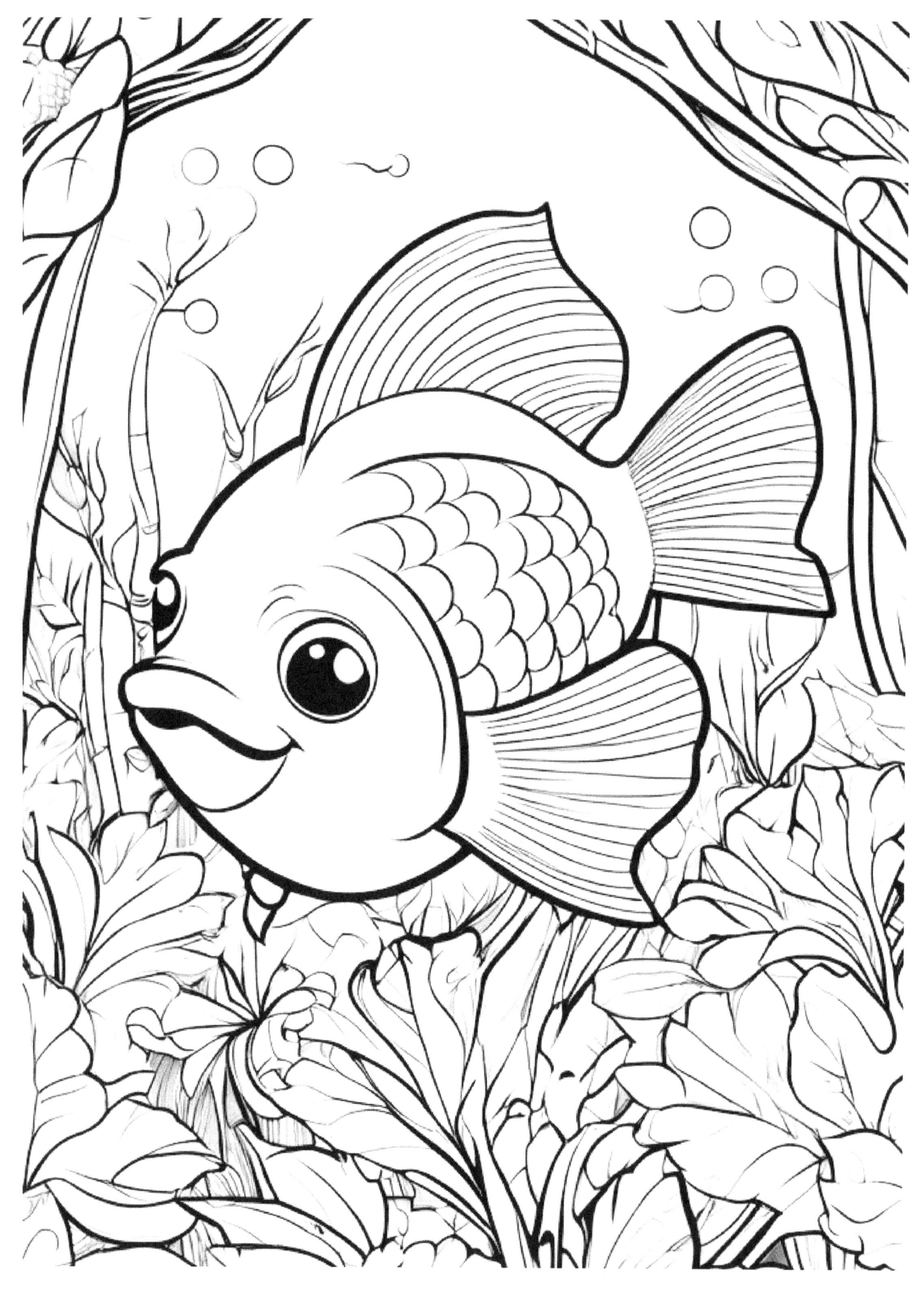

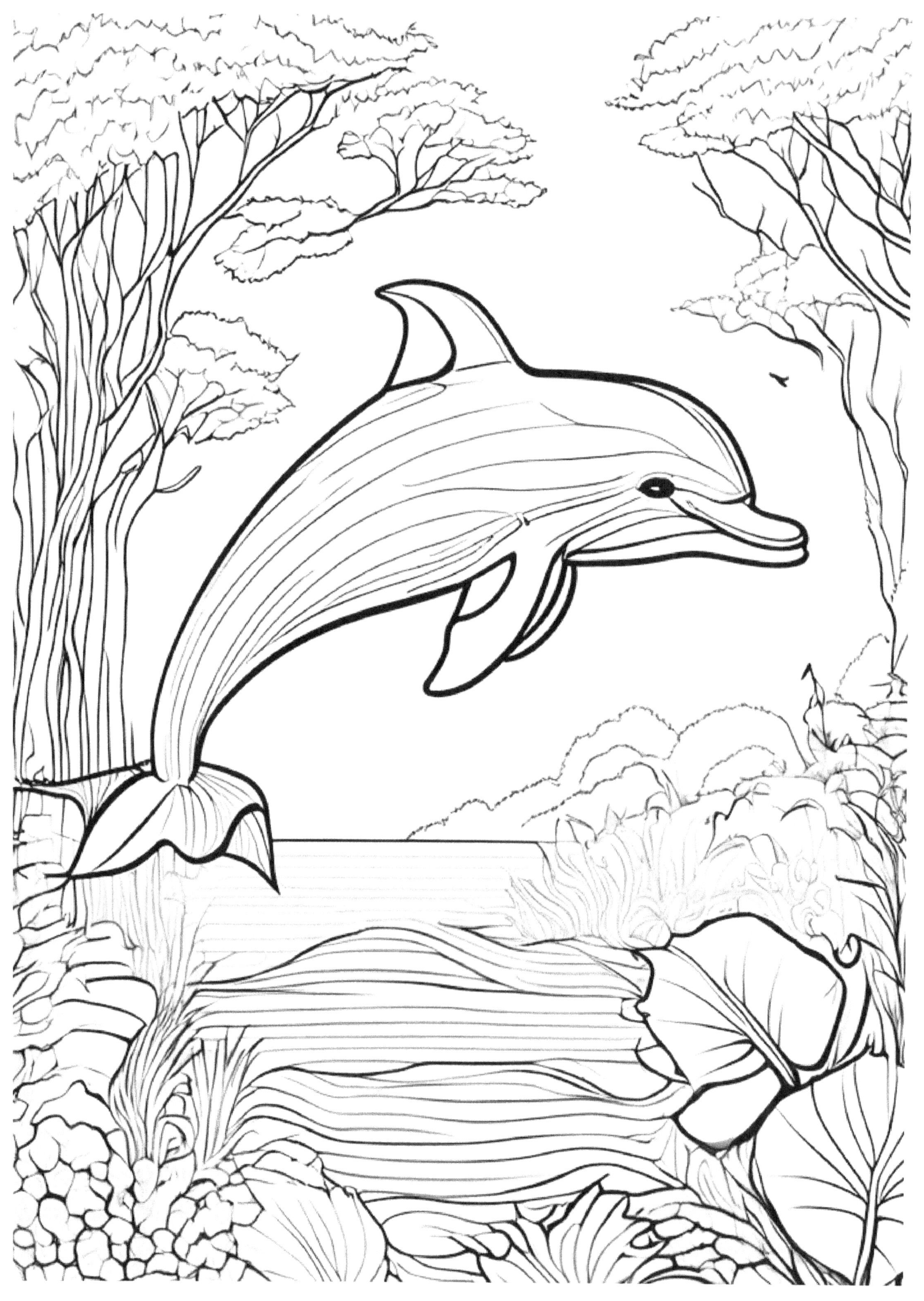

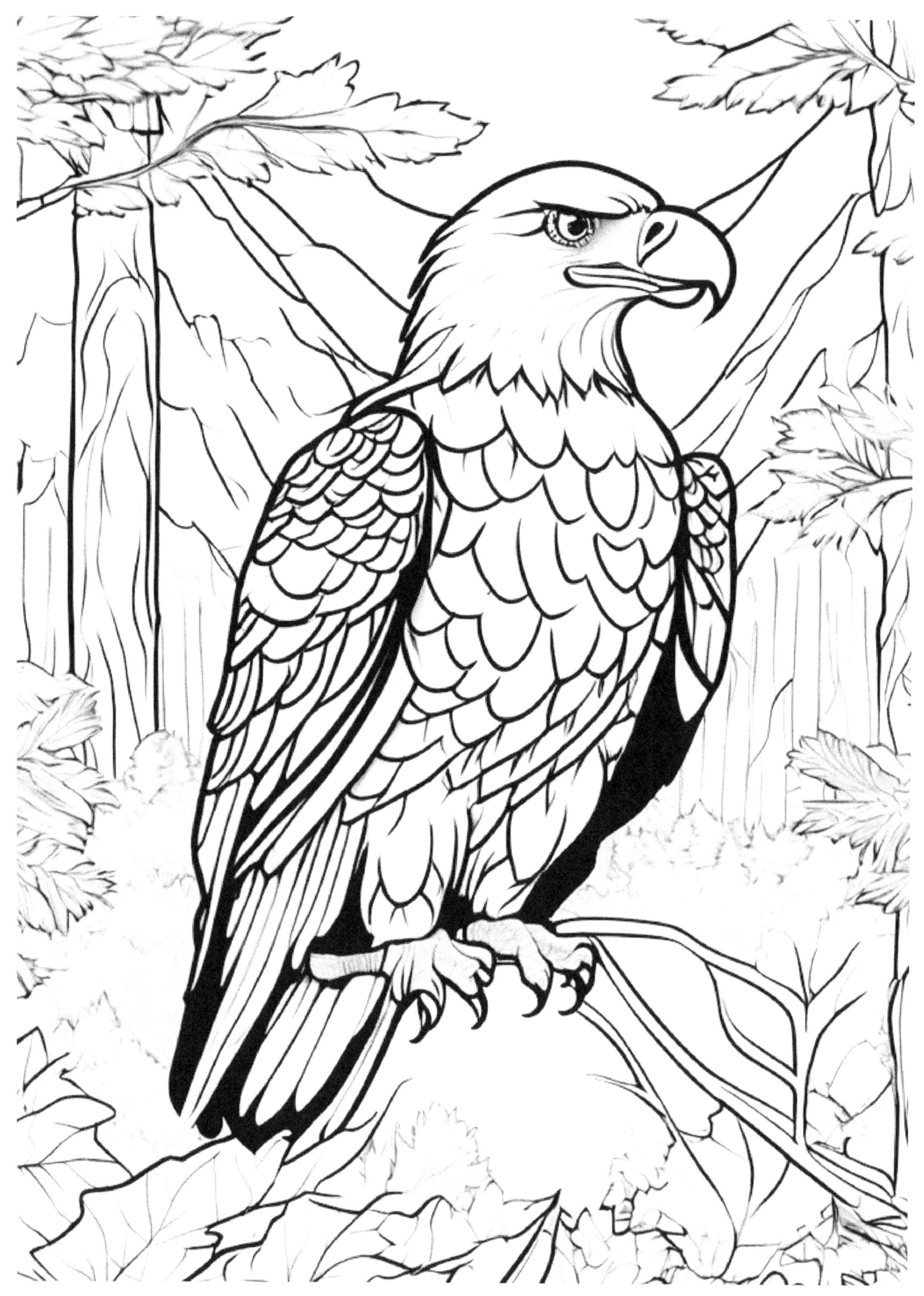

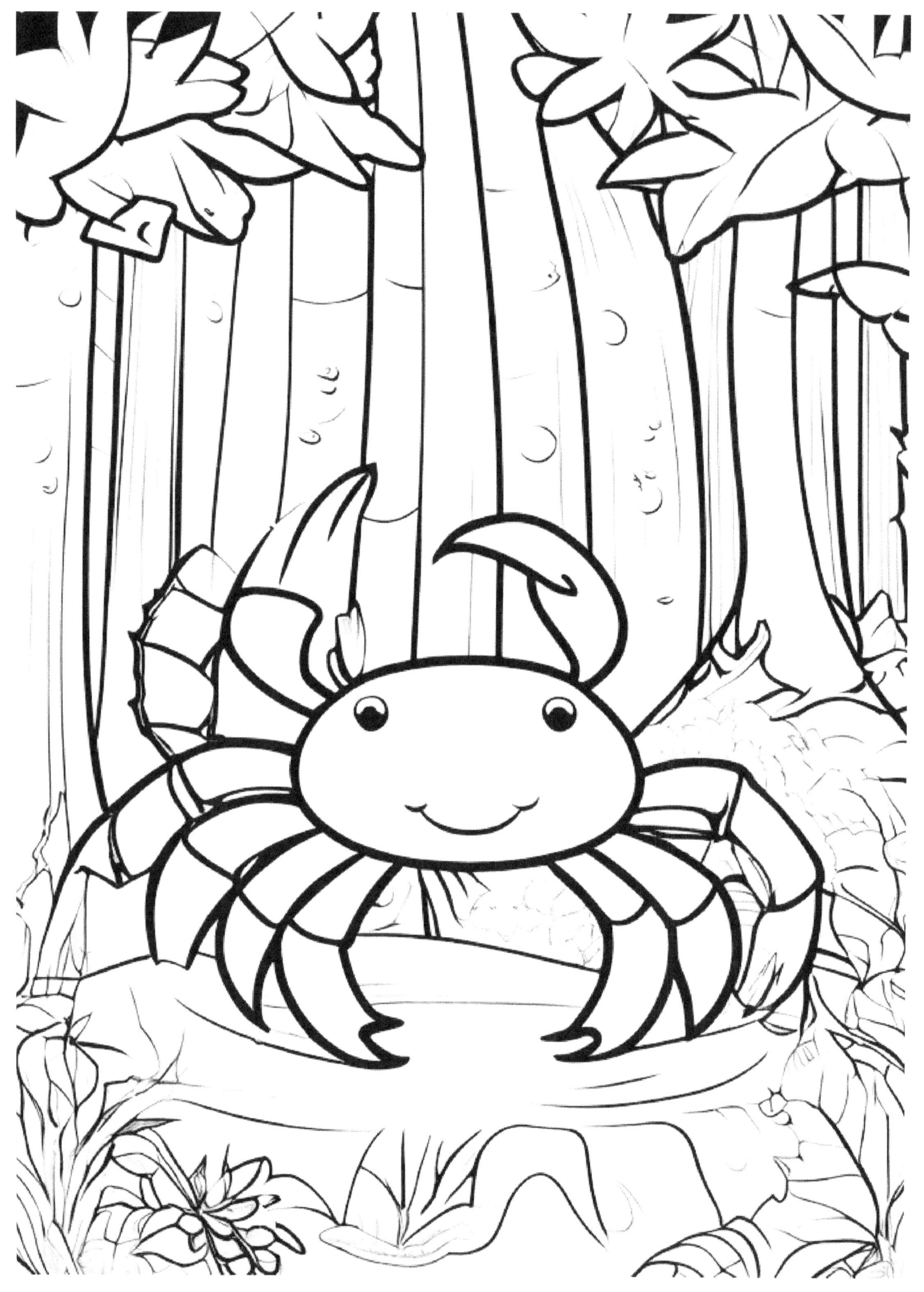

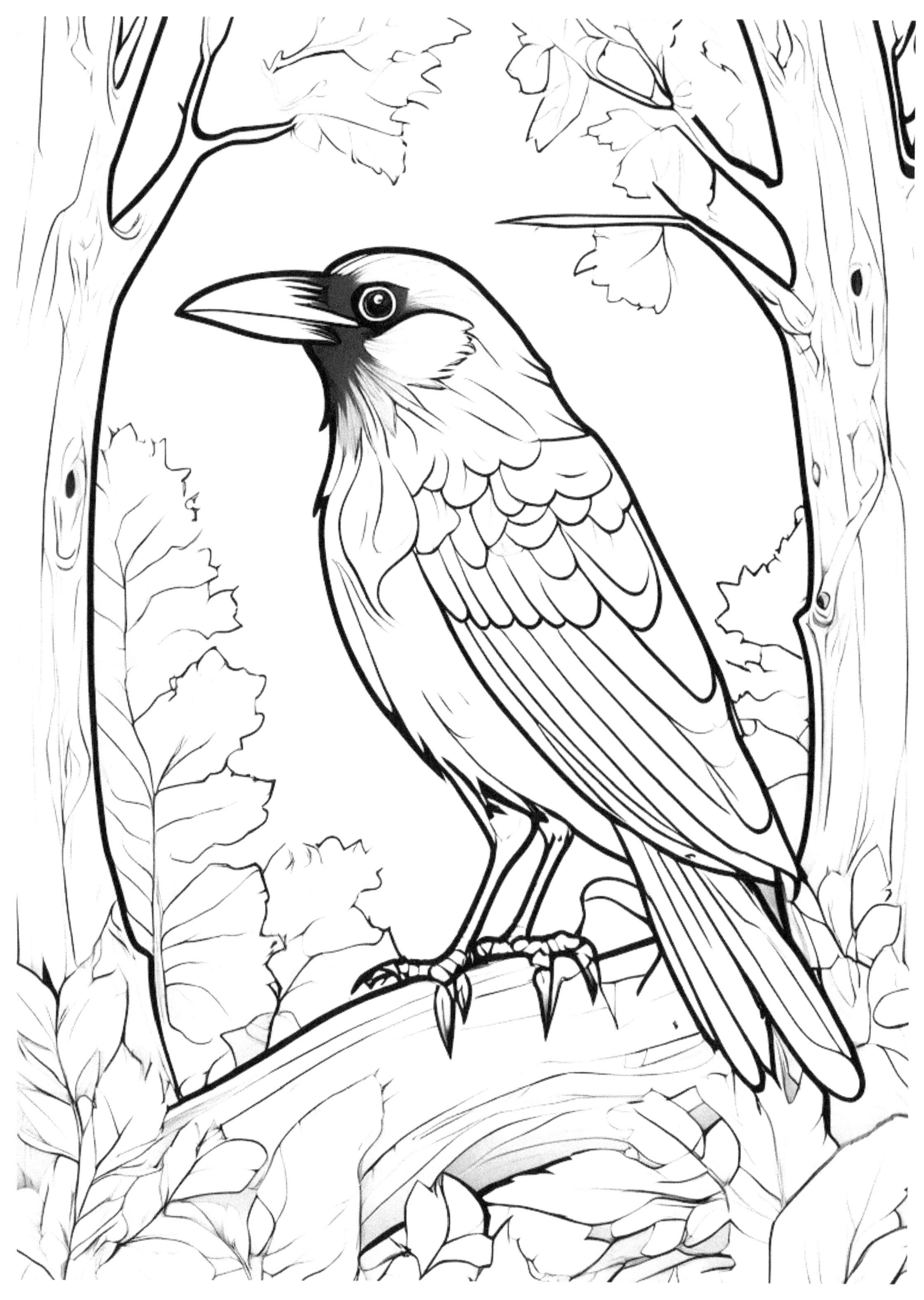

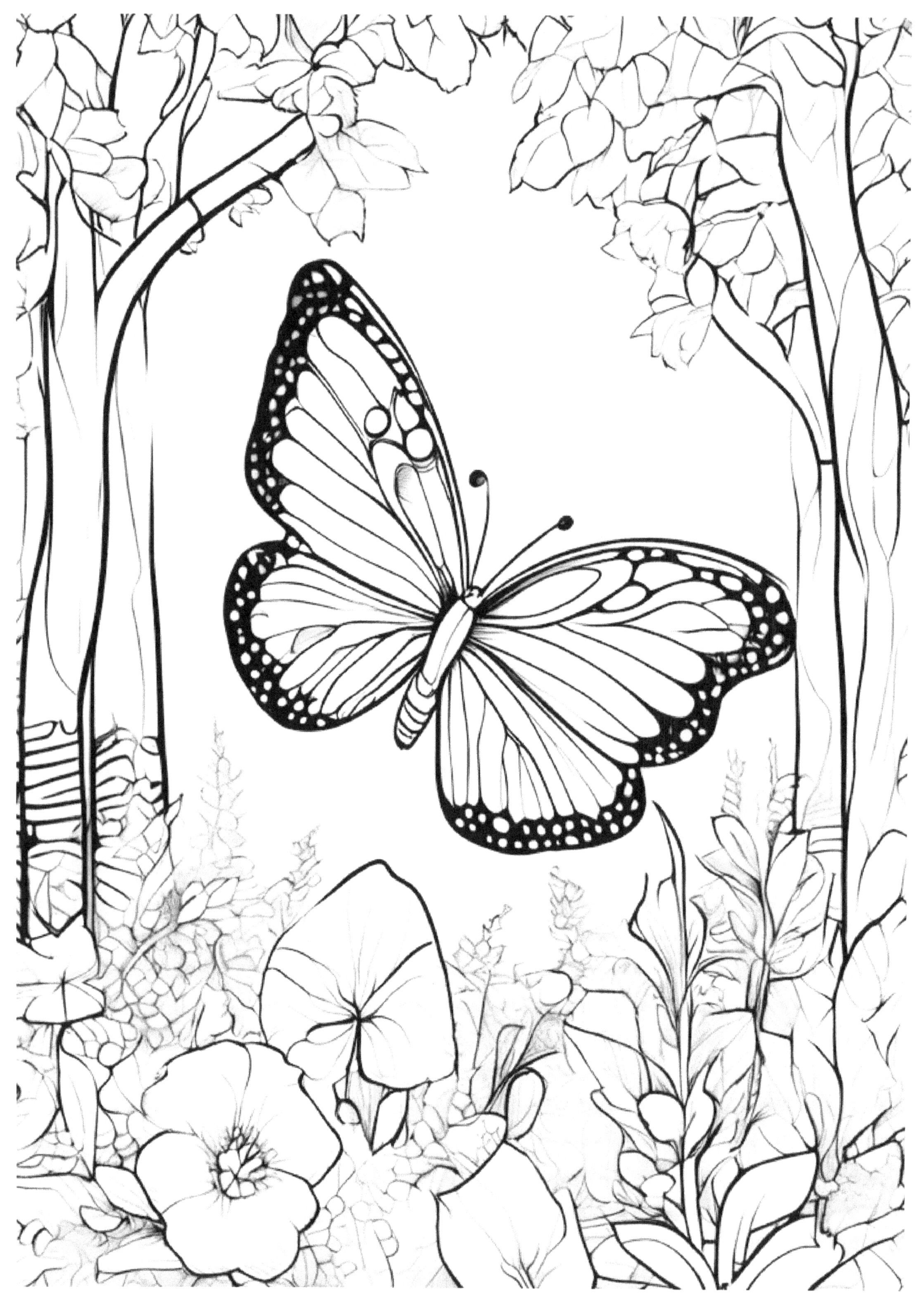

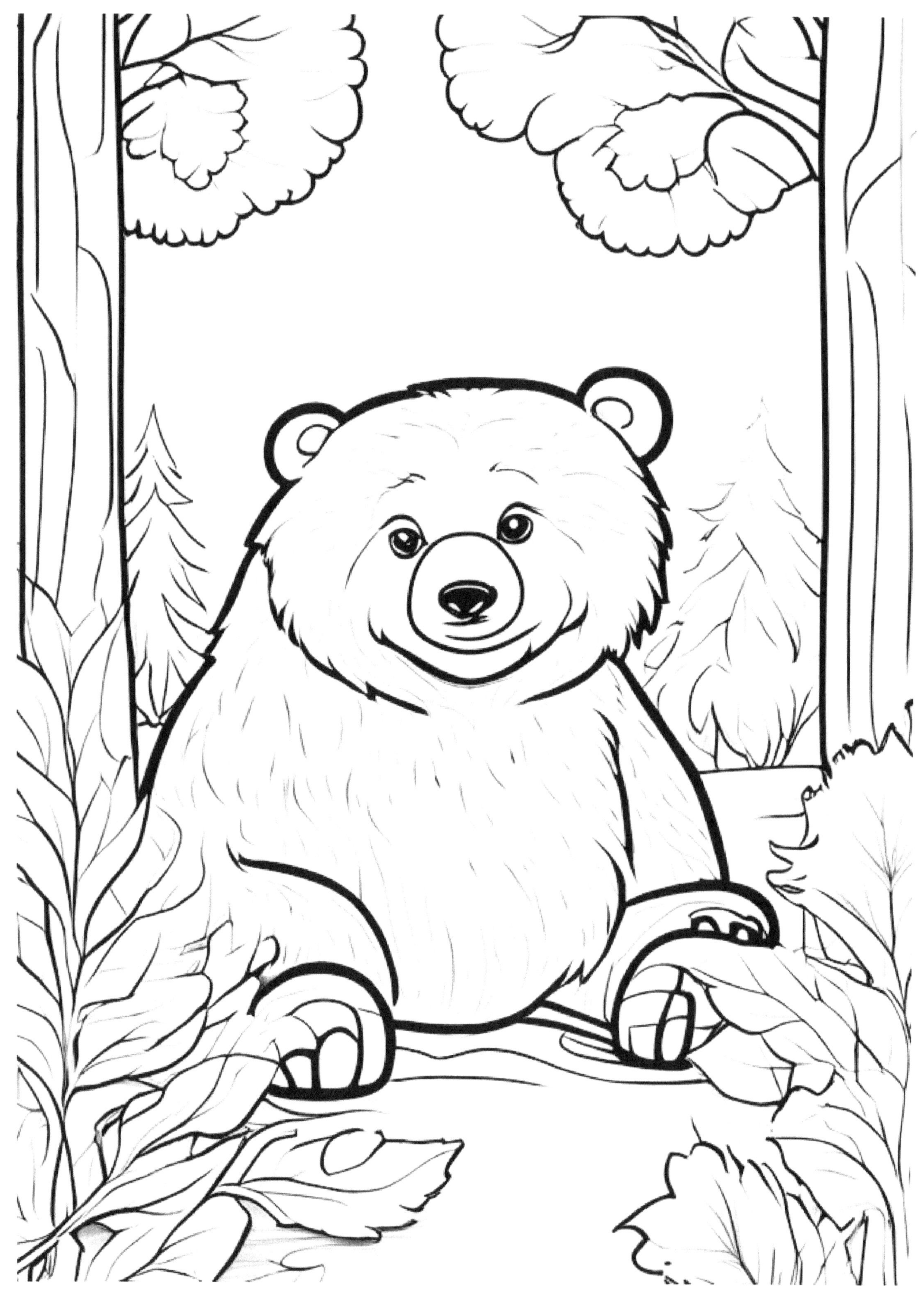

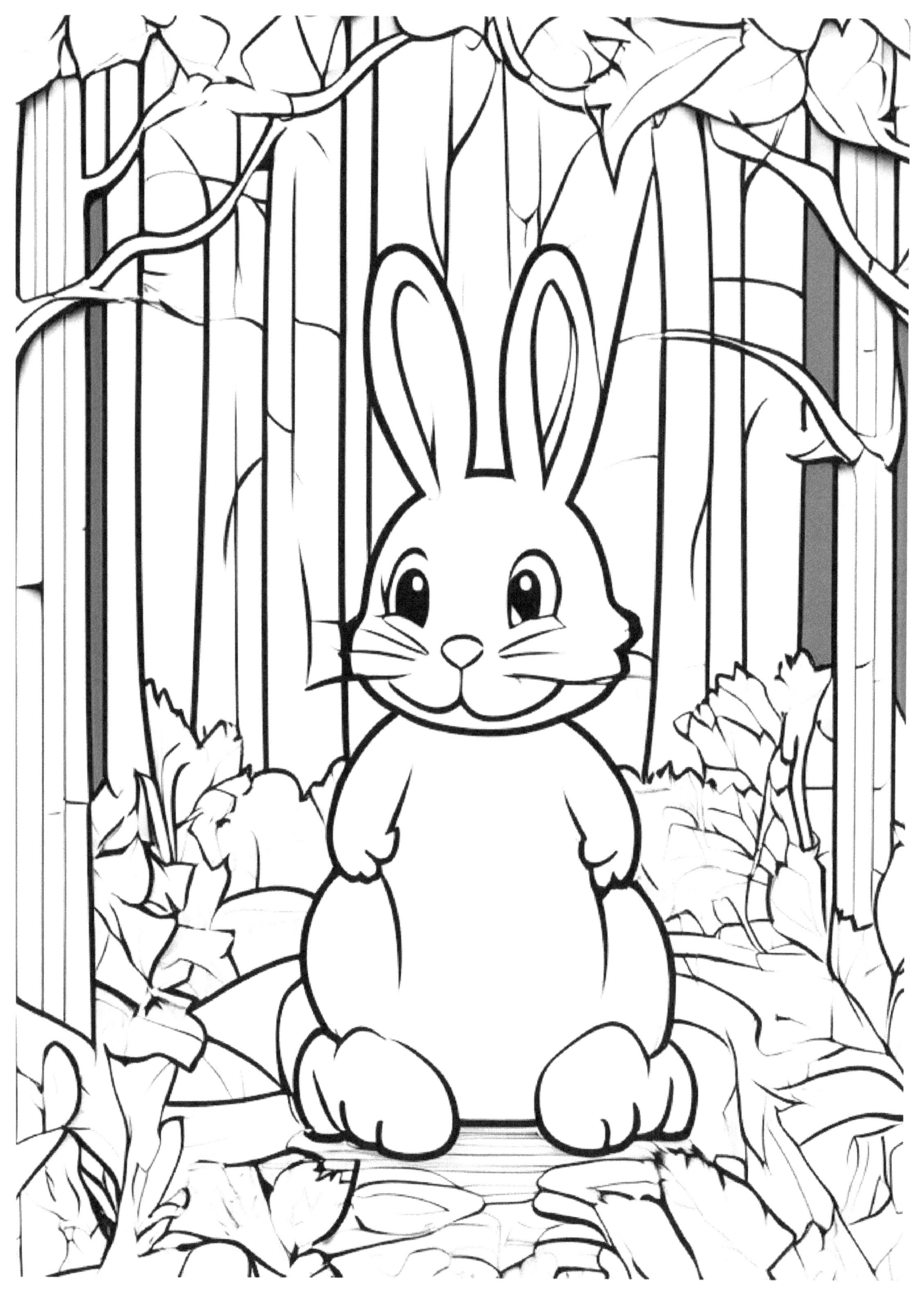

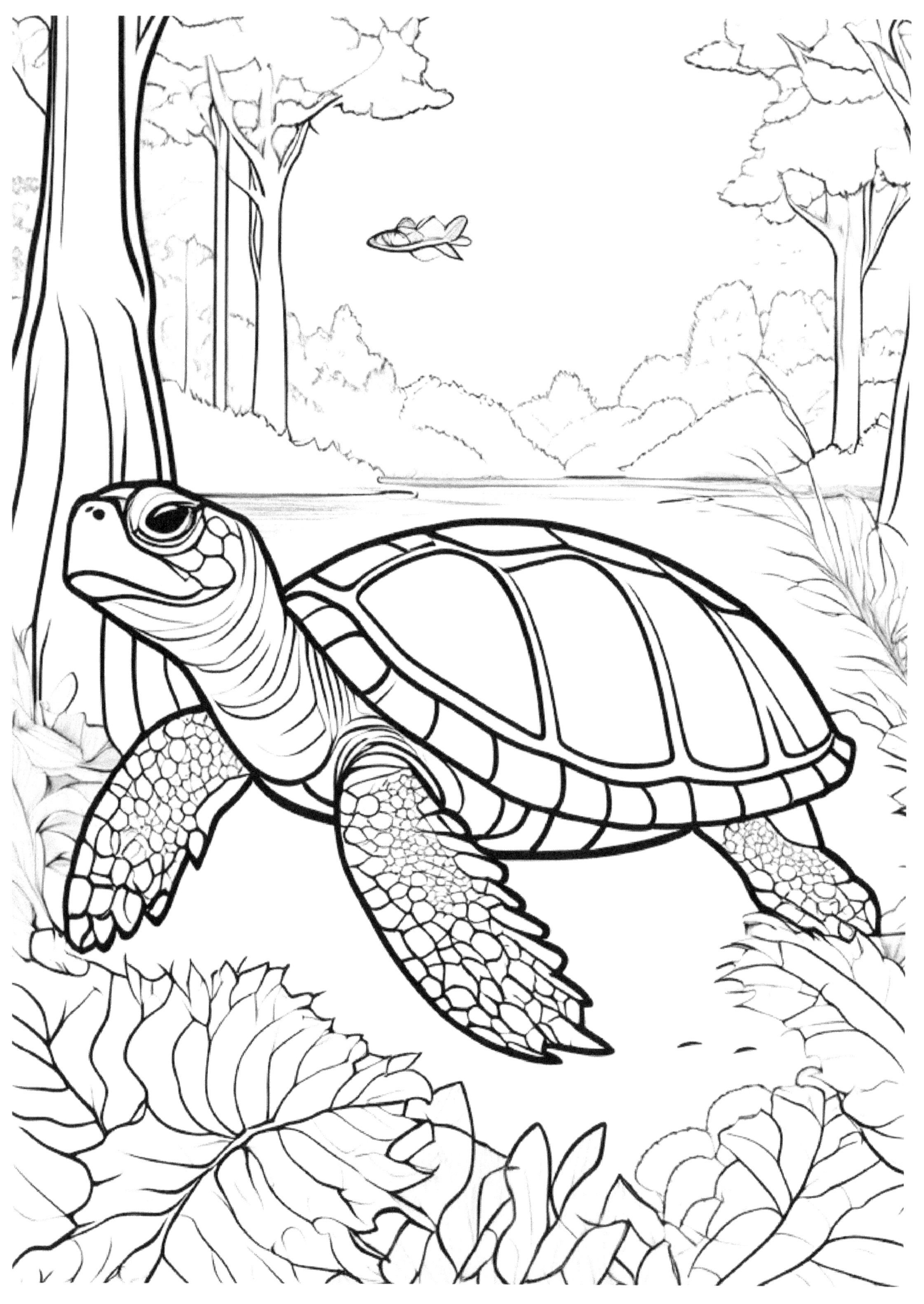

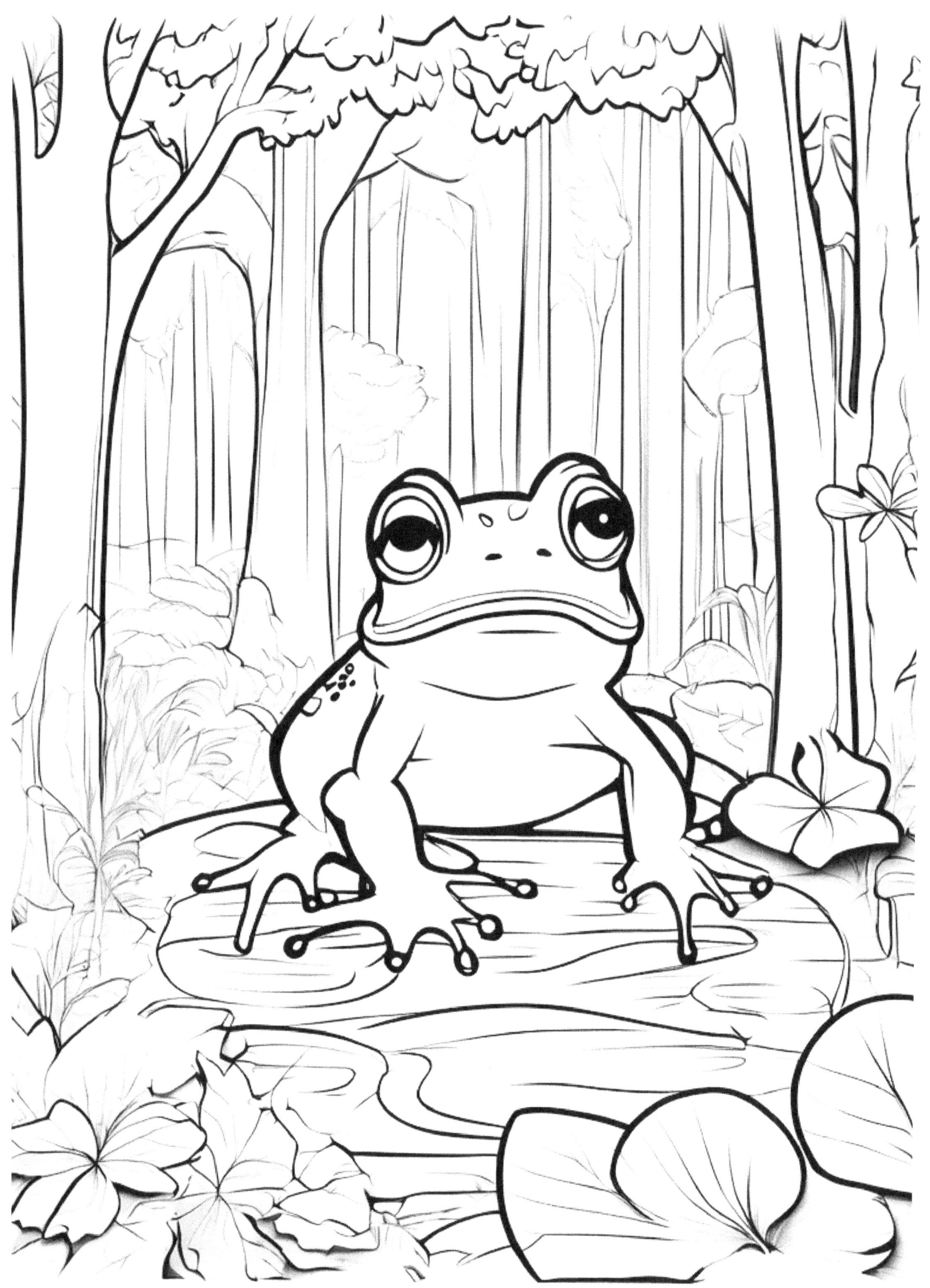

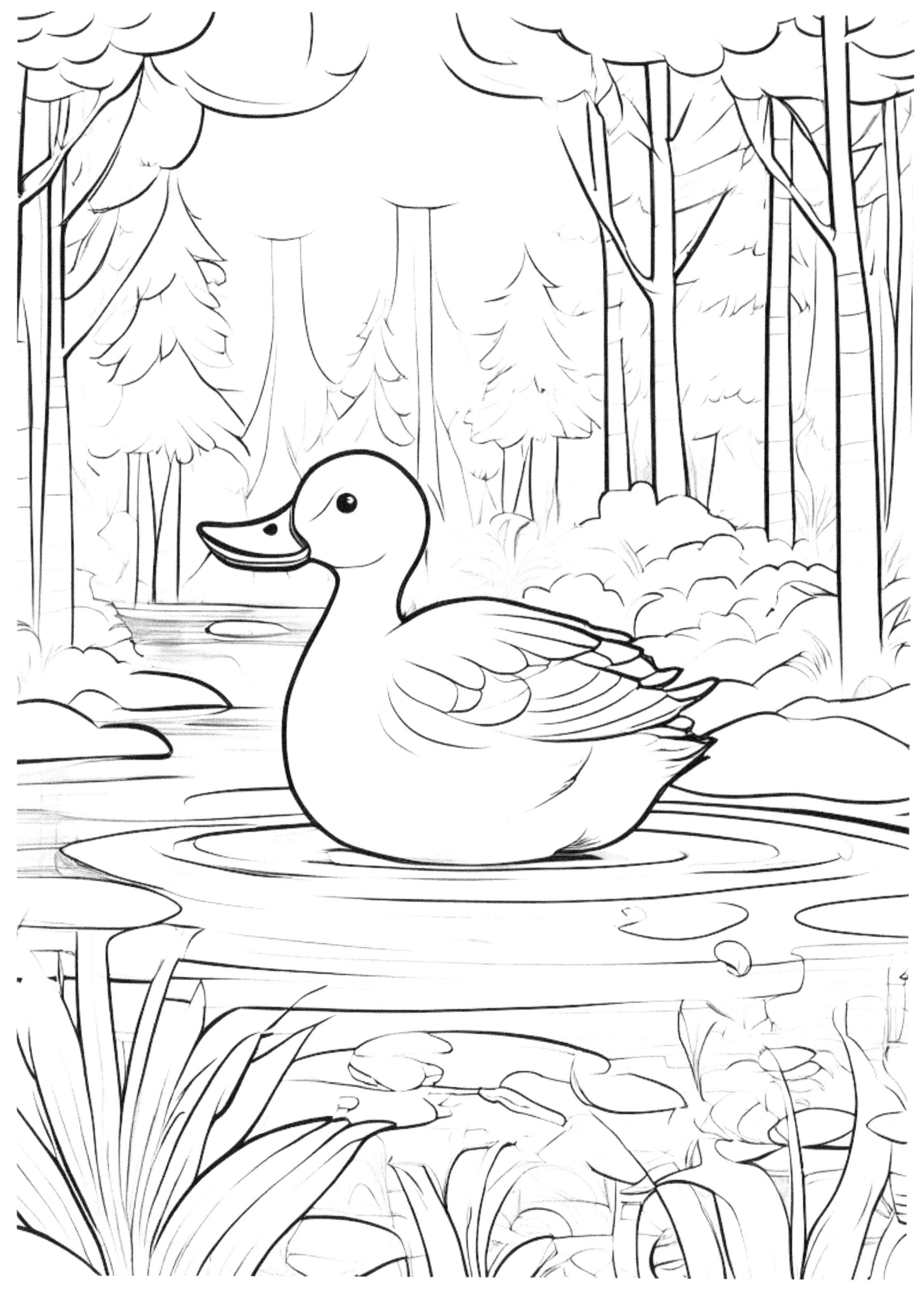

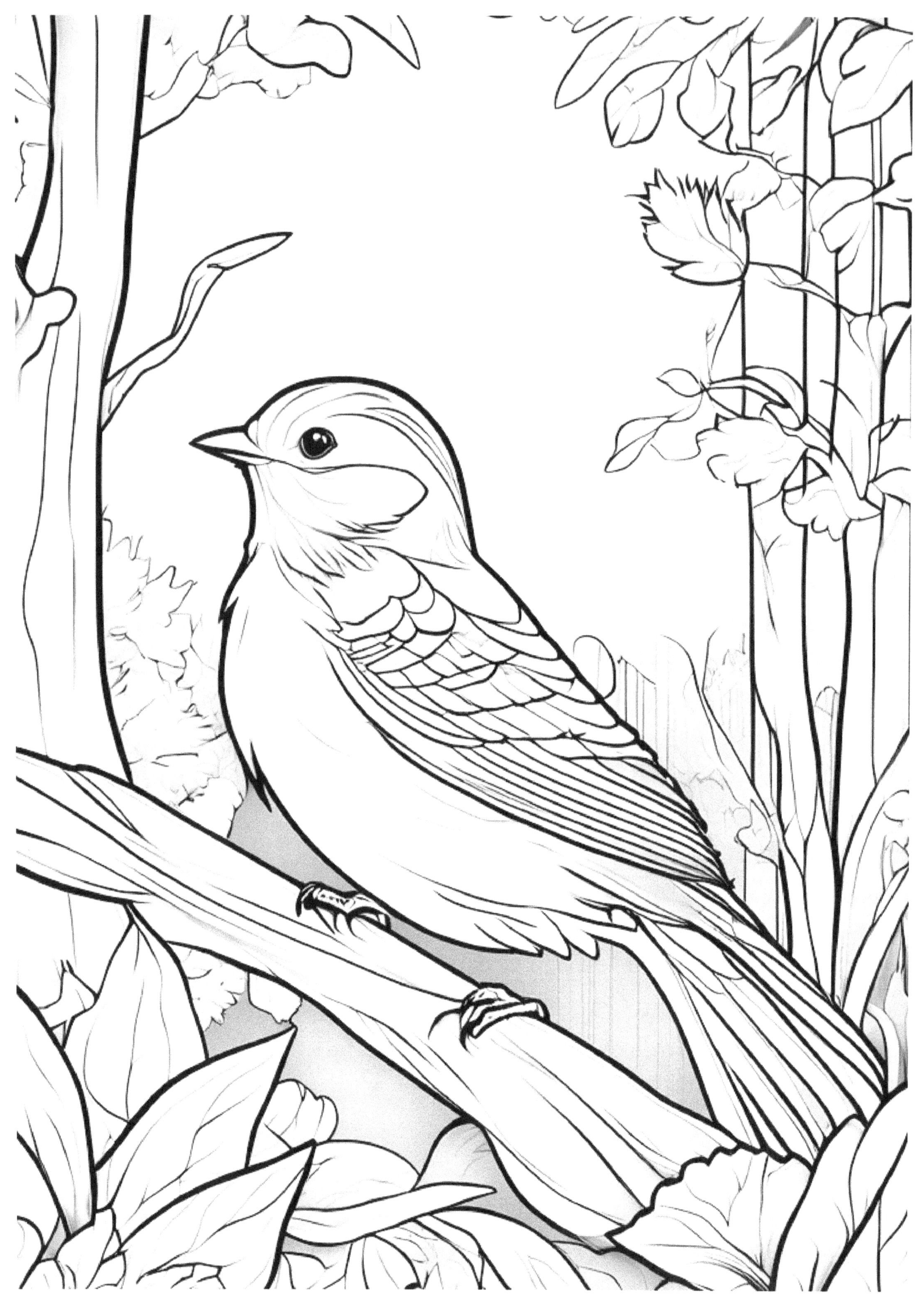

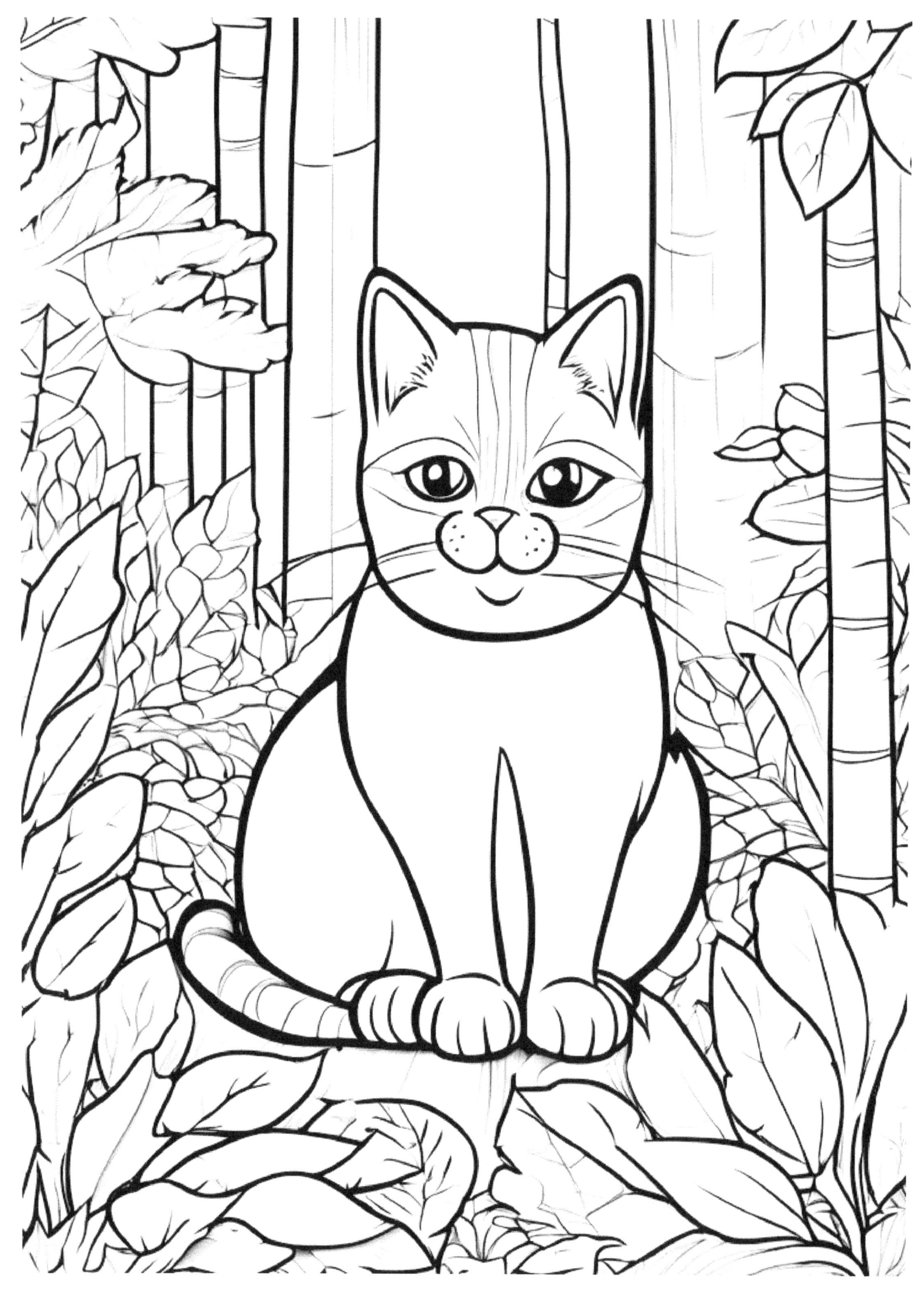

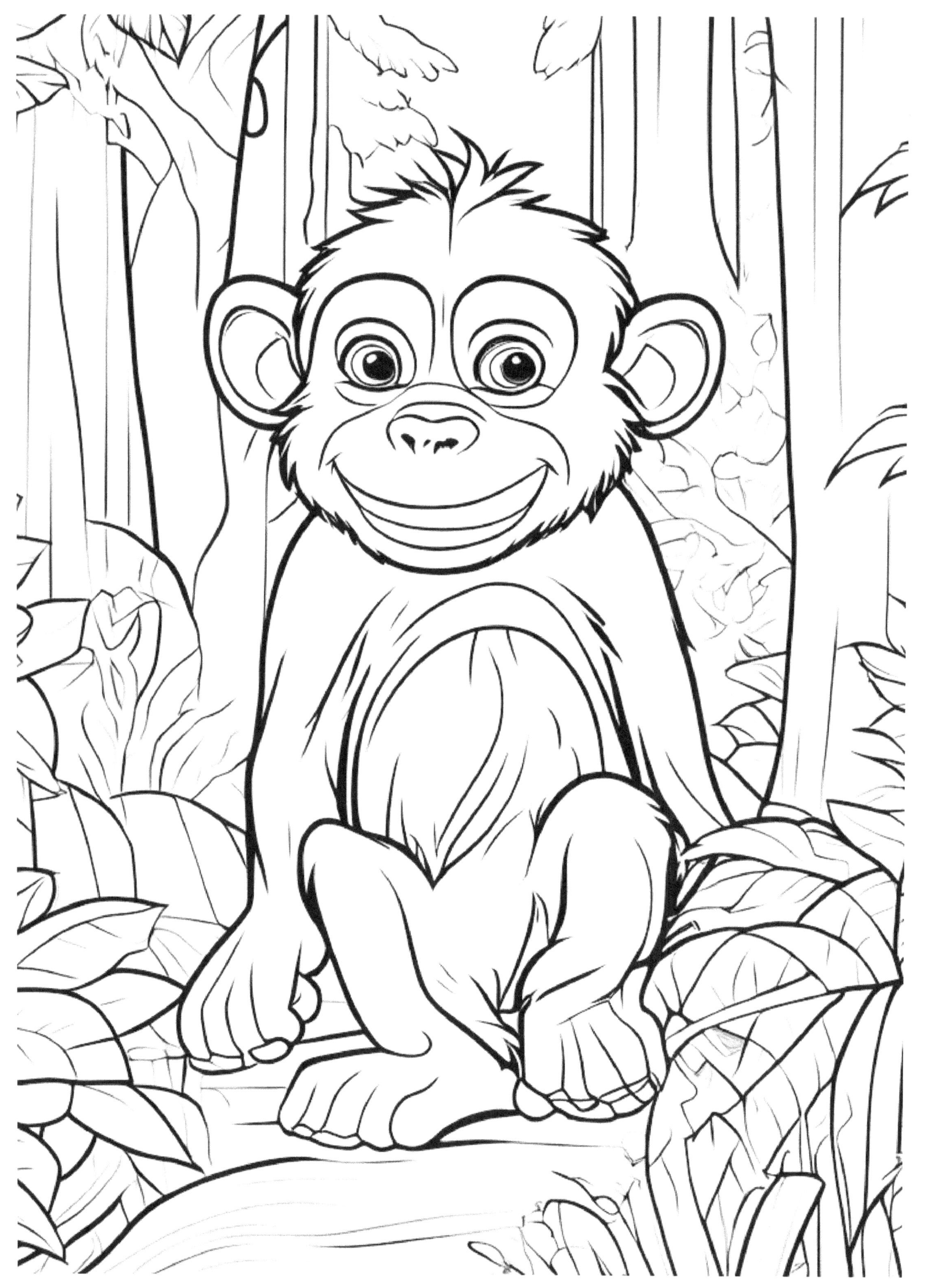

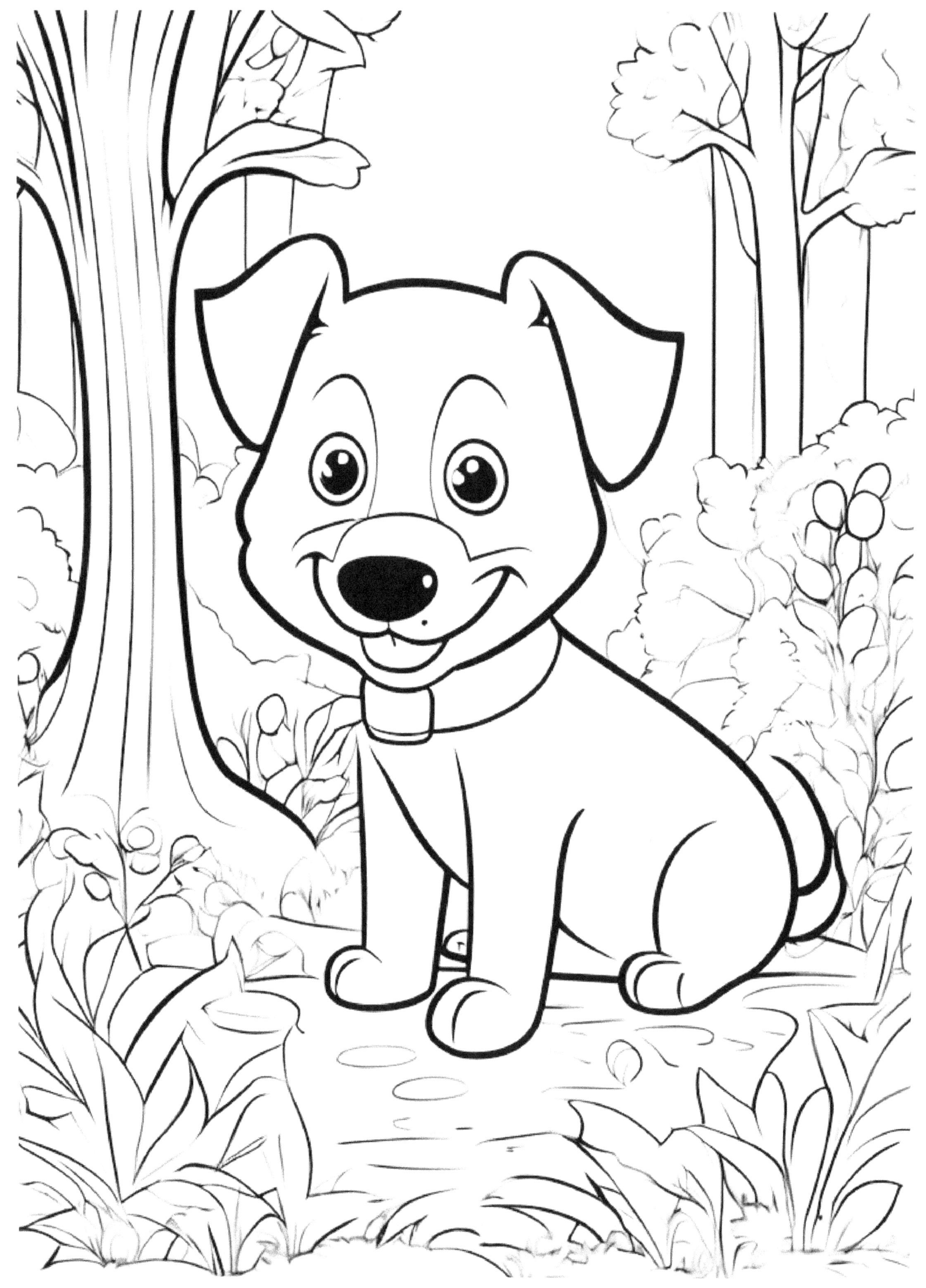

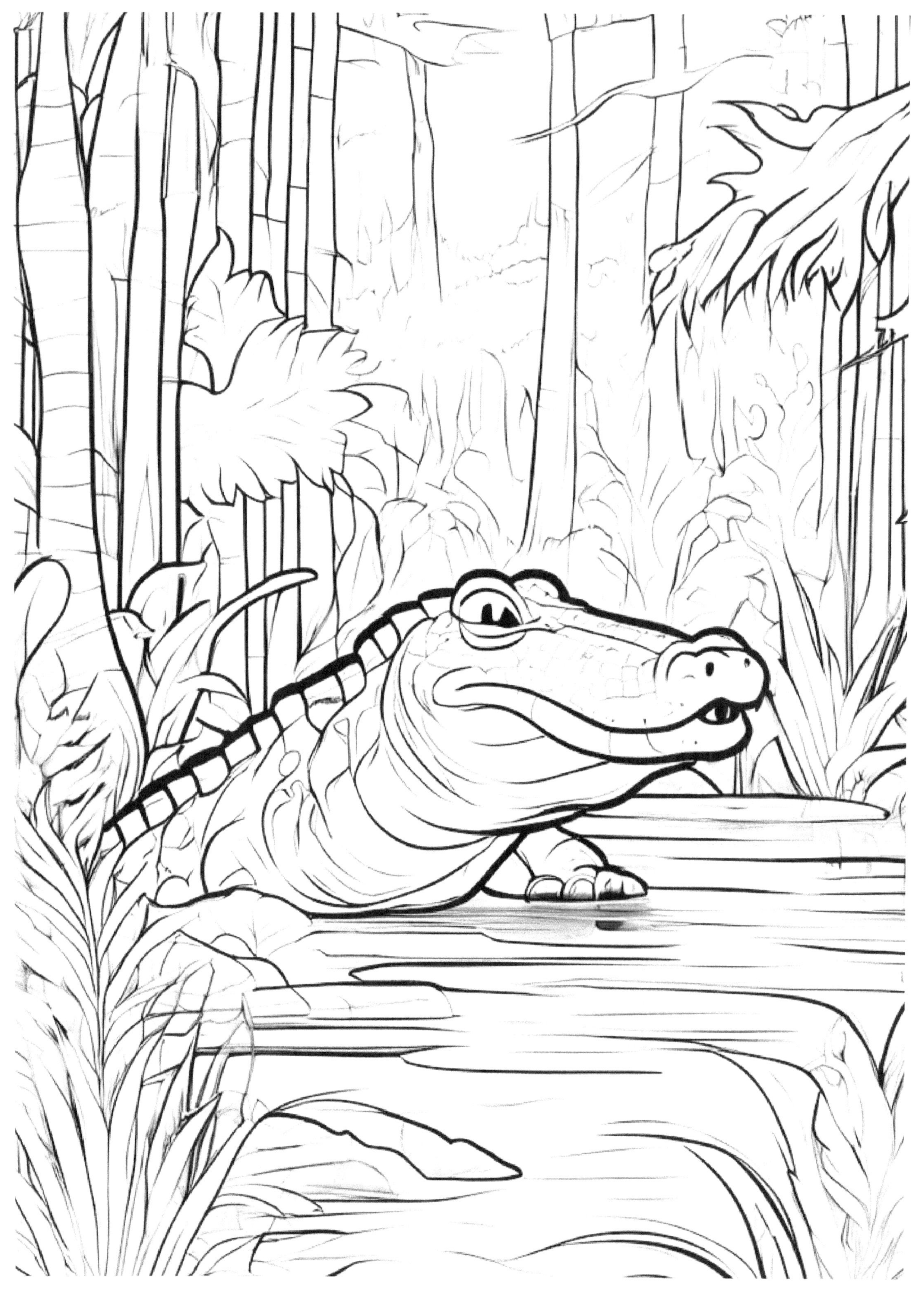

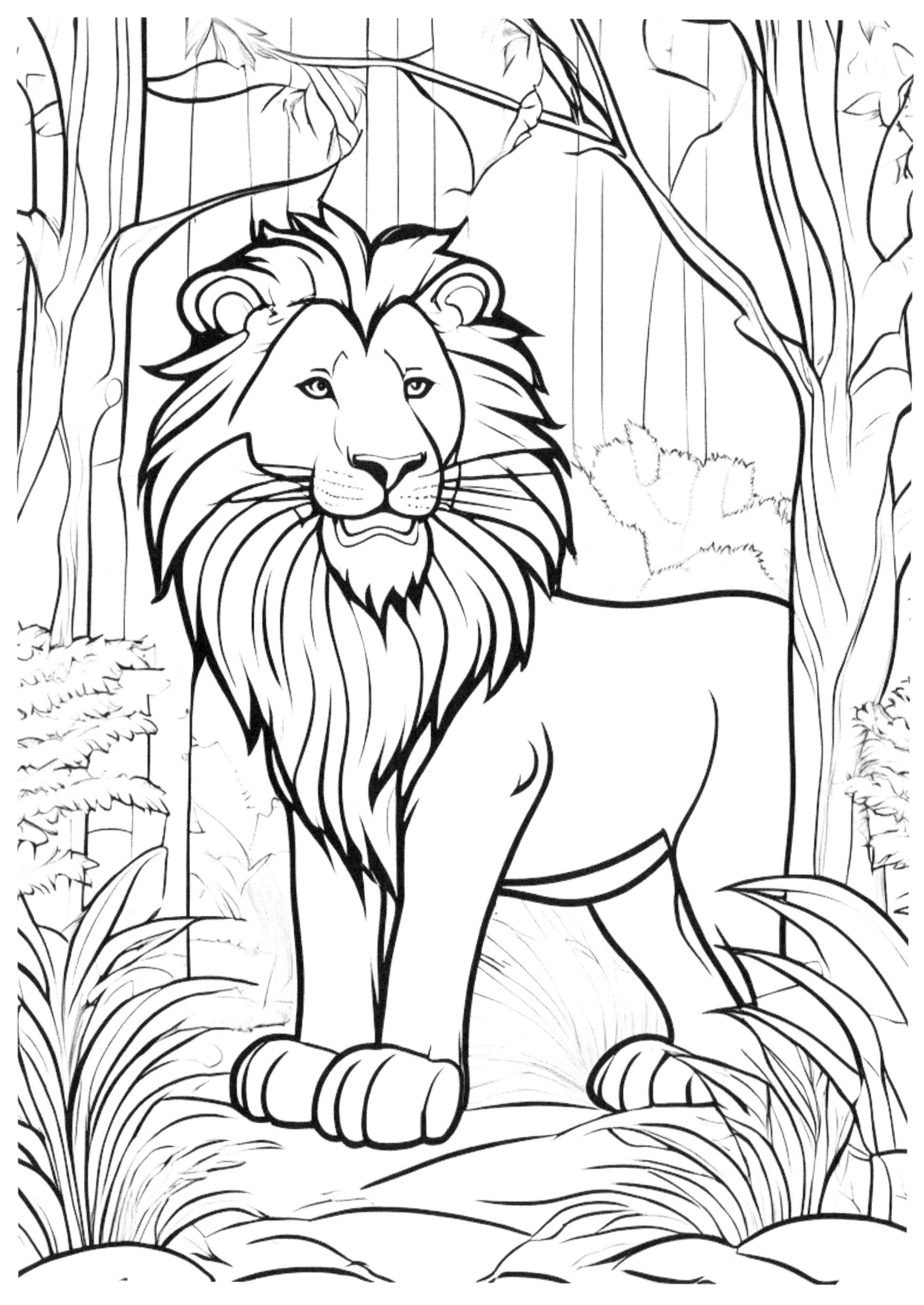